About the author

Psychotherapist and workshop facilitator Matthew Campling, MA (Psych), BA Hons (Counselling), is based in London, England. For over 20 years he has combined running a therapy practice with a prominent media profile, as magazine agony uncle and television and radio guest expert. This is his third book. He is currently writing a second book on this system, *Love, Sex, Relationships and the 12-Type Enneagram*. Contact Matthew at www.12egram.com.

Other books by this author:

Eating Disorder Self-Cure
Therapeutic Weight Loss

MATTHEW CAMPLING

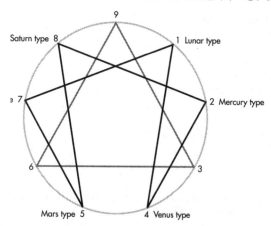

THE 12-TYPE ENNEAGRAM

KNOW YOUR TYPE.
IMPROVE YOUR LIFE.

WATKINS

Sharing Wisdom Since
1893

This edition published in the UK and USA 2015 by
Watkins, an imprint of Watkins Media Limited
19 Cecil Court
London WC2N 4HE

enquiries@watkinspublishing.co.uk

Design and typography copyright © Watkins Media Limited, 2015
Text copyright © Matthew Campling, 2015

Matthew Campling has asserted his right under the Copyright,
Designs and Patents Act 1988 to be identified as the
author of this work.

1 3 5 7 9 10 8 6 4 2

Typeset by Donald Sommerville

Printed and bound in Europe

A CIP record for this book is available from the British Library

ISBN: 978-1-78028-818-5

www.watkinspublishing.com

Contents

For my teacher
and his teachers

PART ONE

You and the 12-Type Enneagram

Chapter 1

Introducing the System

It is often difficult to understand the ways in which others think, feel, and behave. One of the first great realizations of the growing child is the dimly dawning awareness that other people see things differently. As well, much of the time, we can't even understand what drives our *own* thinking, feelings and behaviour. It all seems random and unpredictable. Over the centuries, from Babylonian astrology to Jung, various insights and systems of organization have been advanced to explain human differences. The interesting construction overleaf is what the 20th-century teacher G I Gurdjieff popularized as the 'Enneagram', a nine-pointed figure that soon attracted many different interpretations. This book will reveal some of the fascinating and highly practical secrets that are revealed through having the keys that unlock this seemingly opaque hieroglyph.

Previous to this book there have been several interpretations of the Enneagram which put forward the idea of *nine* personality types. What these nine-type interpretations share is a misunderstanding of the Enneagram figure itself, as you will discover in the quote from Gurdjieff that follows shortly. It is advisable that anyone who has already encountered a nine-type interpretation puts aside the interpretation they know and receives the knowledge in this book as entirely new. Later, when you know more about the 12-Type Enneagram, you can compare the two systems and judge which contains the true message from the past.

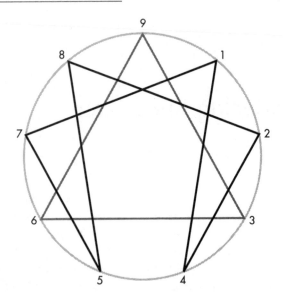

Why Not Nine Types?

Many interpretations accept that each point on the circle represents a human type. And since the term Enneagram means 'nine-pointed diagram', it seems logical that there should be nine types. So why 12? The answer is that the diagram itself is more subtle and complicated than it first appears: the Enneagram is *not* a single, nine-pointed hieroglyph, but is actually *three* independent, interacting figures.

The three figures, and what they represent, are:

- **A circle:** wholeness; the *all*; no beginning and no end; space/time continuum.
- **A six-pointed figure:** the six basic human essence types. These are centered, radiating outward, *being* types. As well as the six main types, there are six *hybrid* types. The six hybrid types are *becoming* types, in motion on the lines between the six main essence types. Hybrid types contain traits of both the type they have just left, and the type towards which they are heading.
- **A triangle:** these points are *not* human types; they are Cosmo-Personal Forces affecting all humanity:

    3 = shocks of earth & fire = affects basic drives
       = underworld

6 = shocks of water = affects emotions
  = the sea
9 = shocks of air = affects thought
  = Heaven/higher-self

It is crucial to realize that the six points and the three points belong to *two separate constructions*, not one. In P. D. Ouspensky's book, *In Search of the Miraculous*, he quotes Gurdjieff:

> The circle is divided into nine equal parts. Six parts are connected by a figure . . . Further, the uppermost point of the divisions is the apex of an equilateral triangle linking together the points of the divisions *which do not enter into the construction of the original complicated figure* [p. 286, my italics].

Treating every point that touches the circle as a different type destroys the priceless message of the Enneagram diagram and despoils the meaning of the 'magic number' series. This number series is derived from a stunning mathematical process, as will shortly be explained.

For now, if we consider the different points on the circle (1 to 9), we notice that the 'original complicated figure' involves only six numbers: 1, 2, 4, 5, 7 and 8. What is the meaning of this? If we remember that each of the six numbers represents a human type, a comment from Gurdjieff (again quoted by Ouspensky in *In Search of the Miraculous*) enlightens us:

> In order to understand the Enneagram, it must be thought of as in motion, as moving. A motionless Enneagram is a dead symbol, the living symbol is in motion [p. 294].

What is alive, awaiting us are the type forces on the Enneagram. But if we move from 1 to 9, on the outside of the circle as some have advised, we are subjecting ourselves to the 'Law of Accident'. The conscious path, the 'Way of the Sly Man' that rescues us from the randomness of the 'Law of Accident', is something that requires much more thought (for a glossary of system-associated terms visit www.12egram.com).

The key to unlocking the secrets of 'moving through life situations' on the conscious path, lies in enlightened use of the ancient principle that every Wholeness can be divided into seven parts. (For example, there are seven days in the week, Newton divided the colour spectrum into seven colours, there are seven different-letter notes in the musical scale, people hailed the seven wonders of the ancient world. Seven was always the number of Wholeness, of Completion, of the 'Everything'.)

So, if we divide the number 1 (wholeness), by the number 7 (complete parts of wholeness), something amazing happens:

$$1 \div 7 = 0.142857 \text{ recurring}$$

Only these six numbers appear in the answer no matter how far you carry out the division. *And they continue to appear in the same order.* These six numbers – each of which represents a human essence type – reveal the potential conscious life-path of every individual person who exists. We all are anchored in one of the numbers (our essence type) or somewhere on an Ennegram line between two numbers (a hybrid type is 'less stable, more changeable' because they have the influence of two consecutive main-type energies). And we can move through the numbers of the 1–4–2–8–5–7 series, only by moving *inside the circle.*

To realize fully the extraordinary nature of this number series, simply do this:

multiply the basic number 142857   by 1 = 142857
by 2 = 285714
(same numbers, in same order, but different start)
by 3 = 428571
(same numbers, in same order, but different start)
This happens until you multiply   by 7 = 999999

This represents 'completion'. It does not advance further. Therefore we are concerned only with the first six progressions.

Introducing the Planetary Type Names

To simplify the discussion of the six basic essence types we will assign planetary names to each number in the 1–4–2–8–5–7 series. To explain where these cosmic entities enter the picture is not within the scope of this discussion. The next chapter will describe the characteristics of each type in detail. For now, just realize that when we speak about numbers or planetary names we are referring to the following:

1 = Lunar type   (142857 x 1 = 1–4–2–8–5–7
           is the path of Lunar type)

4 = Venus type   (142857 x 3 = 4–2–8–5–7–1
           is the path of the Venus type)

2 = Mercury type   (142857 x 2 = 2–8–5–7–1–4
           is the path of the Mercury type)

8 = Saturn type   (142857 x 6 = 8–5–7–1–4–2
           is the path of the Saturn type)

5 = Mars type   (142857 x 4 = 5–7–1–4–2–8
           is the path of the Mars type)

7 = Jupiter type   (142857 x 5 = 7–1–4–2–8–5
           is the path of the Jupiter type)

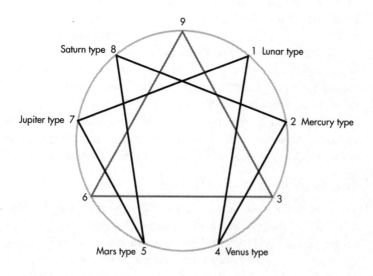

All of us are meant to journey through these secret Enneagram paths from the moment we are born. We start in Lunar-type and follow the 1–4–2–8–5–7 path to (4) Venus (consciousness of the other, of 'mum'), then to (2) Mercury (consciousness of everything in the outer world), and so on through the rest of the number sequence. At some time in our early years, we begin to settle into our real essence type, our 'home type'. This often happens around seven years of age – but some people enter their essence type much earlier. It is then that the Enneagram path begins to be crucially important to our development.

Explaining the Planetary Types

These names have been associated with astrology for millennia, but we are using them in a purer, simpler sense: our language has absorbed the truth of each planetary entity to some extent. We call people who are fast-acting 'mercurial' (from the planet Mercury); those of a deep and introverted nature 'saturnine' (from Saturn); those with jolly, warm dispositions 'jovial' (from Jupiter). Therefore, this 'secret knowledge' has been hiding in plain sight and has been revealed to anyone perceptive enough to look at the obvious: we have been identifying people as having the characteristics of the Moon, of Venus, Mercury, Saturn, Mars (martial arts) and Jupiter. We just did not understand the profound significance of what we were seeing.

The Enneagram not only shows us the six basic human essence types, but also provides a map of the 'Enneagram Path', which is an explanation of how each of the six types should journey through an entire life, through a single day, or even a single hour. The Enneagram Path is the key to all meaningful change, to all-important knowledge of ourselves, our relationships, and our growth potential. So the mathematical path that leads us to these unfolding truths is the first of our important discoveries.

Our Relationship to the 12 Types

The 12-type Enneagram codifies and depicts the *alchemical influence* of the *planetary force centres*. Whereas the previous nine-type interpretations refer to the nine points as 'personality types', the 12-type Enneagram depicts *essence types*. We are all one or other of the types and in certain individuals their essence type is immediately obvious, as we will discover. But human nature is more complicated than our having a single essence type, because *we have all the type-energies within us*. It is this phenomenon that gives us the seemingly random and infinite variations in people, although once we have studied the 12-type Enneagram we realize that all the seemingly infinite variations can be recognized as belonging to one or a hybrid of the six main essence types. (and what is particularly fascinating is to see how the *characteristics are differently interpreted* by individuals). Not only do we need to understand that all the energy types are necessary within us for a properly and fully functioning life, we need to realize that, with these, all the different and specific working energies we need are present and accessible. The consequence of this statement is that it Is vital that we have extremely specific and accurate definitions of these different energies, so as to allow us to develop each of them consciously within us. This is central to the purpose of this book: to set down comprehensive information on how to recognize, interpret and apply the information available through the Enneagram diagram.

A Brief Personal Background

There are three elements at work in this book: knowledge, interpretation and application. The knowledge, the actual *system*, originates from a higher source and is not 'mine'; it has been passed on to me by my teacher, Ron Clairmont. Many years ago I studied in his school of esoteric knowledge and learned about the existence of the 12 types. As far as is known, over the last 40 years this knowledge has been available only through my teacher's school. In 2012 he invited me to write a book about the 12-type Enneagram, and this is the result. My teacher has shared with me some marvellous papers, on various aspects of the knowledge, which he wrote for students in his school, and at various points throughout the book the essential information has come directly from him, including much of this introductory chapter. Additionally, in order to convey an impression of how the different types manifest and move through life, I have compiled lists and broken down the application of the system into different sections and chapters. It must be emphasized that some of this interpretation is mine and that a different author might interpret differently. However, inclusions such as the speed of different types, the three divisions into which the six main types fall (intellectual, emotional and moving), the symbols of the types, and other knowledge as distinct from interpretation are all part of my teacher's knowledge. To conclude this paragraph of personal background I would like to acknowledge the valuable contribution of my teacher's associate, Eric Walstedt.

The Full 12 Types

A particularly powerful feature of the 12-type Enneagram is the way in which my teacher has distilled the seemingly random and infinite variety of human behaviour into a few highly specific and meaningful words (listed below with **main types** in **bold**, *hybrids* in *italics*).

Note that whenever we refer to one of the essence energies we add 'type' – for example 'Venus type', not 'Venus'. This is because the term refers to a type of energy associated with the planet, not the planet itself.

1	**Lunar type** – Childlike, Intuitive, Innocent, Trusting
1 & 4	*Lunar–Venus type* – Childlike Adult, Sensual, Affectionate, Vulnerable
4	**Venus type** – The Languorous Lover
4 & 2	*Venus–Mercury type* – The Busy, Fun-Loving Lover
2	**Mercury type** – The Busy-body, Business/Comedian type
2 & 8	*Mercury–Saturn type* – The Busy Thinker
8	**Saturn type** – The Philosopher–Creator
8 & 5	*Saturn–Mars type* – The Socially Active Thinker, Power-Driven Planner
5	**Mars type** – The Athlete–Warrior, Sportsman
5 & 7	*Mars–Jupiter type* – The Humanitarian, 'Benevolent Forcefulness'
7	**Jupiter type** – The Jolly, 'Feeding' Parent, Giver, Peacemaker
7 & 1	*Jupiter–Lunar type* – Fairytale Friend–Parent–Child

To repeat: The numbers on the 12-type Enneagram do not represent the planets as such, but the influence of the planetary force centres.

Parents encourage their children to develop in a particular way, not appreciating that the way may not be type-appropriate. Many of us enter into relationships and perhaps marriages that are challenging in unexpected ways, because of the essence types involved, and, later we may find we are torn apart by 'irreconcilable differences'. Consider the people you have known over the last 10 or 20 years. Have you wondered why some people's lives become so messy and 'tragic'? The intellectual, top-of-the-class boy who suffers a traumatic breakdown in the cruel world outside the safe school walls, the 'successful' father or mother whose children hate them fiercely for their insensitive, controlling demands. And those who drift from one job to the next, apparently making every effort, but being rewarded only with failure and defeat.

But once we know which type category we belong to, we can learn to use the specific talents of our type, and we can try to avoid the known pitfalls of our type. As we learn more about type characteristics, we learn to value other types for their particular talents, and we learn to forgive them for their predictable inadequacies. Ultimately the purpose of this book is to teach the reader a path of transformation – a path that leads toward the happy, successful self you could be. Transformation of the self is never easy, but it begins with trying to learn the truth about who you are, what your essence is, and how you can relate most successfully to others.

In the following two chapters we will attempt to explain the secrets of each of the six main types and the six hybrid types, expand on how the influence of the different energies gives rise to who we are, what we value, and how we use or waste our talents.

Chapter 2

Introducing the Six Main Types

Recognizing Your Type

The names of the six major 'essence types' are the names assigned to the planets nearest us – plus Luna, the moon. The characteristics associated with these heavenly objects are already familiar to us through mythology and references embedded in our everyday language:

Mercury	Mercurial personality (indicating quick, sudden bursts of spontaneous thought and movement)
Venus	love, beauty, sensuality; venereal (referring to the sexual organs)
Mars	Martial arts (combative, physical)
Saturn	Saturnine (in older meanings, dense, secretive, unreadable features and behaviour)
Jupiter	Jovial (warm, jolly personality)

There is no question that people use these words without even realizing they are speaking about ancient Greco-Roman gods. Why then have these word associations persisted in our language (and in many other languages) – is it not that there is some irrefutable, observable truth behind the association?

The one problem comes with words relating to the Lunar type. Unfortunately 'lunatic' or 'loony' are the words most commonly used to describe the influences of the moon on people. However, 'moonstruck' behaviour has its good and bad aspects. Creativity is thought of as a 'lunar' activity: the moon inspires us. And what might seem to be a liability, 'the *changeable* moon' is often a blessing to the Lunar type: whenever they are in a bad mood, most of the time they will change quickly, and not even remember what was bothering them.

Introducing the Six Main Types

In this chapter we will explore the six main-type energies and in the next chapter we will examine the six hybrid types. It is crucial to understand that although we have only one 'home' essence type, we have *all* the type-energies in us – and we may manifest different type-energies at any time. And for reasons that will be explained in later chapters, some people behave differently from how their essence type would predict. But in general, the correspondence is amazing.

Studying the type-energy forces helps us to discover hidden assets and abilities that we can use to transform our lives. We can learn to develop the natural talents and avoid the unfortunate pitfalls inherent in our essence type. The 12-Type Enneagram gives us the tools to understand ourselves, and those around us. Also, knowing that some potentially undesirable qualities are intrinsic to certain essence types, we can begin to view those 'faults' with compassion and new insight. We can appreciate and forgive others, and when necessary, learn to appreciate and forgive ourselves.

As you read on about the types, try to associate each one actively with someone you know. Later, we will find that the Enneagram actually tells us secrets about each of us as we travel its strange, jagged paths. But for now, try to absorb the basics, and vividly imagine the people being described. You will know you are making progress when you have a sudden flash of insight into your own, or someone else's, previously inexplicable behaviour.

The Six Main Essence Types

These descriptions are direct from my teacher.

Lunar type (1)
Definition: Childlike, Intuitive, Innocent, Trusting

Kind and spontaneous, eternally naïve, independent and creative, the Lunar type sees things simply and – to them – clearly. Think of a small bird, a blackbird or a robin. The quick flick of the head and the delicate way it flits from bough to grass to wall: Lunar type movement patterns are like this. Attracted to bright, primary colours, to anything that's 'fun', they shy away from adult responsibility. They create their highly subjective version of 'reality' by indiscriminately processing information as if every impression they input from the world is equally valid. They then accept this medley of fact and imagination as their 'truth'.

Lunar types – one of the two intellectual types on the Enneagram – live in their minds. Their intelligence is basically intuitive, and they will often, like children, surprise those around them with a profound insight. However, they often lack the ability to explain the path of logic behind their conclusions. Sometimes they will spin off into an obviously unfounded private fantasy that only they seem to understand. They regard their idiosyncrasies as badges of their 'independence', signs of their 'uniqueness'. They often choose to wear odd clothing and accessories that would look ridiculous if any other type wore them. But their choices don't seem ridiculous – just 'unique', and this creative approach to life extends into everything they do.

Lunar types are prone to confusion, and stubbornness, but they can be extremely grateful for guidance from a person they regard as 'a wise friend'. Lunar types will usually begin stories or explanations with 'I' – I think, I feel, I believe. They may not grasp the significance, but they think of themselves as children and often live in a self-obsessed, inward-looking cocoon. They often have a desperate need to feel connected to the rest of the world. What they need most is not someone to 'love' them, but mostly someone to pay attention and 'understand' them. However, when they attract attention from people they don't know well, Lunar types sometimes become nervous, and overwhelmed. They may then sabotage the opportunity, by becoming giddy or bratty, or they may just shrink and 'disappear' into their own world. They seek out relationships in which they can be parented, 'looked after', because, like children, although they imagine they are independent, they are in fact highly *dependent*. Lunar types often seem to be telling you their ideas, when actually they are simply seeking approval, because secretly they do not trust their own thoughts.

Their inner stubbornness will occasionally cause them to act senselessly. They are prone to paranoia and worry needlessly about things that are never going to happen. At the same time, they often neglect attending to genuine life issues. And when they do address real problems, they can easily become overwhelmed. Just as children can occupy themselves for hours in 'playful' behaviour, so as adults, Lunar types seem to play their way through life. But, overwhelmed Lunar types can become suddenly angry or hostile, and then, just as suddenly, act as if nothing had happened. Easily disappointed in the real world, they can become profoundly negative: 'hell is other people'. But oddly, the Lunar type can face a series of disasters, and, unlike any other type, they can recover their cheerfulness and resourcefulness almost immediately, and then they refocus and rescue themselves with immediate actions to fix the situation.

A most important characteristic of the Lunar type is their incredible ability to forgive themselves and others. A Lunar type will often survive an abusive parent and emerge with far fewer scars than their siblings. And lastly . . . no other type matches the Lunar for childlike, disarming charm.

Venus type (4)
Definition: The Languorous Lover

Imagine a fish gliding sensuously through water: that's a Venus type at a party. Venus types devote a lot of time and money to perfecting their personal style. Creating beauty becomes their main mission in life, and all the other types, if they are wise, consult the Venus type for advice on what clothing to wear and how to beautify their homes. Venus types respect 'designer' labels and anything that indicates 'luxury', yet they also know how to make clothes and home decor look 'expensive' even when they are not. Their attire and grooming are impeccable and appropriate and, like no other type, they manage to relax easily in any surroundings. Wherever they are, they seem 'at home' and comfortable. Even as children, long before the other types mature, the Venus type radiates a personal confidence that makes them look and feel like adults in an adult world.

Although Venus types are concerned with their appearance, they also enjoy 'unwinding', 'putting their feet up'. They normally don't like physical exercise unless they have a personal trainer 'relationship' to motivate them. They would rather spend time flicking through a glossy fashion magazine, enveloped in a cloud of romantic music, or sitting in the garden in the warm sunshine (but not *working* in the garden). And nothing trumps the pleasure of lounging in a scented bath. The 'languid', earthy characteristics of the type make them prefer to be the still centre around which everything else revolves. Even when they are alone, everything in their environment 'relates' to them, and seems to exist for their benefit. The waters of the bath and the garden sunshine are welcomed as friends that have come to soothe them. Imagine the difference between a Lunar type at a party, anxious over who is and is not their 'friend', compared to a Venus type who considers she or he is the centre of everyone there.

Venus types are manipulative, and make many attempts to control their partners and friends – mostly because they want to see if what they are doing is a winning manoeuvre. Oddly enough, unlike most other types, if their manipulative gambit works, they often instantly reverse tactics and become submissive and loving. And also, oddly enough, they respect and enjoy being manipulated by someone they like. Most of the other types manipulate people for a reason, but to understand the Venus type, you must realize that their version of manipulation involves playing a *game*, a game they do not need to win. It is the game itself that matters. Other types don't understand this since no other type functions this way.

The Venus type is earthy, and enjoys touching. Whereas Lunar types fleetingly touch objects, even the air, with their sensitive fingertips, the Venus type strokes languorously with finger pads: they seem to be learning about the world by touching, and they spontaneously touch their body, touch others, touch beautiful objects, interesting textures – anything that attracts their attention. They love *being touched* and are easily the most sensuous of all the types. They even 'touch' with their eyes, which look directly, deliberately at you and seem to be examining your body, your clothing . . . everything about your physical being.

Other types may misinterpret the actions of the Venus type as an invitation to intimacy: yes, Venus likes to be held and caressed, but only by a chosen partner. The Venus type is often far more physically and emotionally faithful to one love interest than their sensual natures make them appear. To them, a 'love' relationship means everything, cures all and promises all, so they want to preserve it at any cost. They are also extremely loyal in friendships. Venus types will go to enormous and convoluted lengths not to end either a friendship or a love relationship, preferring to try to resolve the problems by talking . . . and talking. A familiar Venus type expression is, 'We've got to talk!' If relationship difficulties cannot be resolved, they don't back out gracefully. The exit ceremonies of Venus types often involve melodramas, and endless speeches about who said what to whom and who is to blame for whatever.

The problems that other types experience with Venus types are sometimes more subtle: Venus likes to talk about 'feelings', and encourages others to 'share' personal information. But the Venus type takes even the most casual remarks seriously and often a careless or misunderstood phrase will cause the Venus type to start accusations, mostly out of context, that begin with 'But you said . . .' However, if you *don't* share personal information with them, Venus types feel they are being 'closed out' of the relationship. If you do share personal information, the Venus type may use it to stir up trouble simply because they never feel more alive than when they are the centre of 'emotional' dramas. Venus types often like to give advice to their friends about their relationships with third parties, and they frequently end up saying to their friends things like, '. . . well, you *should* care – you *should* be upset! You *shouldn't* let 'X' treat you that way!' It never occurs to Venus types that they are constantly, deliberately getting involved with something that does not concern them. And if you try to tell the Venus type that you don't mind what others are saying or doing, the Venus type insists that you *should* mind, you *should* be upset.

Venus type is the first of our two 'emotional' types and whereas the other 'emotional' type, Jupiter type, concentrates on the emotions of the other person, Venus types concentrates on emotion – period. Sometimes, this has unusual benefits. Their friends are accustomed to the Venus type getting its own way, but the Venus type just as often will stubbornly insist on getting what is best for someone else, someone they like. They are wonderfully intuitive about what others might like, and after a long day's work it is wonderful to come home to a Venus type because he or she will be sincerely interested in your day and genuinely fascinated by tiny details that other types would find boring. The Venus type will enjoy making you comfortable, and making sure you are fed, and rested.

The down side of this concentration on emotion may be that this world of feelings comes at a price. Venus type resists change, and sometimes insists that it knows more than you do about what you want. They are not stubborn or insensitive; it is just that their intelligence is filtered through their feelings. A large problem is the attitude of the Venus type toward ageing. Since its ego is primarily tied to physical appearance, ageing is a slow death to them. It is the only thing that makes a Venus type insecure.

But if a Venus type is operating in a healthy way, nothing trumps its concern for you, its willingness to make you happy. There is no other type that cares about every aspect of your life like the Venus type. And the most cultured Venus types can open your eyes to see beauty everywhere it exists, in art, in music, in decor, and even in yourself.

Mercury type (2)
Definition: The Busy-Body: Business/Comedian types

If you consider ants, the way hundreds, possibly thousands, go about their day at a fast pace, efficiently and with purpose, you have a sense of what the Mercury type does well. They are the first of our two 'movement' types, and being 'busy-bodies' that concentrate on the outside world, they are interested in everyone else's business, often in a helpful way. If you want a job done rapidly and efficiently, give it to a busy Mercury type, not a languid Venus type, or an easily distracted Lunar type.

And this leads to an interesting phenomenon: the *Mercury Society*. Mercury is the type ray that is most commonly 'borrowed' and used by all the other types simply because most advanced technological societies are Mercurial societies in which, to some extent, everybody has to work busily, has to conform, has to make quick, almost mechanical decisions. The Mercury Society greatly values commerce and money itself. Therefore the concerns of large corporations and the wealthy people who own them crowd out the needs of non-business types. The Lunar and Venus types have to think and move faster, and no one is interested in their moods and feelings. The person who is a success, in money-making and influence-gathering is the tribe icon: the most important person in the tribe.

Mercurial societies involve engaging countless behind-the-scenes figures in specific roles. Everyone becomes, to some degree, a pseudo-Mercury type. Like the ant colony, business communities would not survive without the support crew: the multi-tasking mothers at home, the teachers at school who prepare children to enter business, the lower-level functionaries in the corporations themselves: secretaries, accountants, janitors and others. There are even supporting roles for the artists and musicians who busily create audio–video products advertising everything from breakfast cereals to political candidates. All of these people must be perfunctorily praised and rewarded as long as they are productive. But the downside of the Mercury type and the Mercury society is that anything or anyone no longer considered useful is discarded.

But let us move away from the Mercury Society and return to a discussion of the single person who exhibits true Mercury essence type: they often have jobs involving sales, computers, publicity, and event-organizing. They are quick thinkers and facile writers but what they think and write about is usually not deep. This type-energy loves to communicate and interact, and always goes out of its way to see what everybody else is doing, and to listen to what everybody else is saying. They are not particularly loyal in relationships and friendships because they like to constantly meet and interact with new people. In general, the Mercury type is drawn to novelty and is always involved with 'the latest' trends. Mercury types go everywhere in town. They know where to buy anything, see anything or do anything. They will visit the latest restaurant, less for the food and more to be able to say they have 'been there'. Now they have the added busy pleasure of being able to post their critique of it on the Internet.

The Internet is the best thing that ever happened to Mercury types. They used to collect books with endless information, but now they can easily bounce from site to site. They love the speed, variety, and novelty of the Internet experience. Not since the printing press have Mercury types had such a wondrous new friend. Mercury types feel personally proud of 'opening the doors' for others, and the Mercury type never wants to be admired, never wants a reward: it is too busy with the 'real excitement' of moving on to the next whatever. But this 'moving on' can be a major problem for the Mercury type in that *they themselves* miss out on the most meaningful, deep experiences that life has to offer. As part of their frantic ant–bee-activities they talk incessantly about the latest thing they have seen, about what is happening 'out there', about what they are going to do tomorrow. Hence by jumping from topic to topic, action to action, they never become deeply involved with anything, and thus life-altering transformative encounters elude them.

The Mercury type in search of new experiences will often volunteer for too much: they will be on the go from dawn till long after dusk – for a Mercury type there are never enough hours in a day. They like to help people *start* tasks, and often this works perfectly, because others are grateful for the beginning push, and don't expect the Mercury type to finish everything for them. But Mercury types can exhibit enthusiasms that cause others to embark on tasks that are beyond their capabilities. And since Mercury types like the idea of being helpful more than they like working through the details, they sometimes leave the person they are assisting in an impossible mess.

This type-energy is 'non-romantic'. Mercury types are extremely self-conscious in personal relationships. They often say or do the wrong thing in intimate moments, and their body may awkwardly twist away from an embrace because they are suddenly embarrassed, or aren't in the mood to be slowed down by Venus-type demands. (Much Venus–Mercury comedy depends on the Mercury type being awkward in love relationships.) Mercury types have superb memory for practical details, but they rarely question the 'meaning' of what they know. They don't realize it, but they rarely 'feel' anything since their experiences mostly involve thinking quickly and moving quickly. However, they sometimes stumble into a life-changing experience if they slow down enough to allow a Saturn type to lead their minds into a place of depth and profound search for meaning. Suddenly, they enter a hypnotic magical world, where everything they have experienced superficially many times before is reborn as something totally new. It is as if their two-dimensional world has suddenly expanded into three dimensions. This may spark a mid-life crisis in the Mercury type as they now realize how much they have been 'missing in life'. And then, the long, slow voyage across the Enneagram towards Saturn begins.

Mercury types are the worker-types in any society. They are perhaps the most indispensible type. Although friendships with Mercury types rarely progress beyond a superficial level, all other types should be grateful for coming into contact with a Mercury type. They often give us the needed 'shove' to begin our careers, to do what we thought we were not capable of doing, and to get out of our lethargy and take the first steps toward the fulfilment of our dreams.

The Lunar, Venus and Mercury types are 'younger' or 'lighter' types than the three types on the left side of the Enneagram: Saturn, Mars and Jupiter. Crossing from '2' across to '8', we encounter the 'older' or 'heavier' types. The Saturn, Mars and Jupiter types look beyond what is, to what could be. They want to shape the world, to delve deeply into thought, feelings and actions. They are concerned with universal, social, political and philosophical life.

Saturn type (8)
Definition: The Philosopher–Creator, Serious, Profound Thinkers, Teachers

When the scholarly mind of the Saturn type is applied to serious endeavour in any given field, the result can be a breakthrough that changes the way the world thinks about all that has gone before. Saturn types, the more profound of our two intellectual types (intuitive Lunar is the other) never stop applying intellectual curiosity to everything they perceive. They are lovers of knowledge for its own sake: 'The unexamined life is not worth living' (Socrates). The most erudite mentor–teachers, the most serious actors, directors, writers, musicians, theorists in the fields of science and philosophy: these are the Saturn types who have made an enormous impact on civilization.

This type views everything in twin lights of meaning and importance. They read books that have something to teach them, and go on 'holiday' to visit places where they spend most of their time in museums. A Saturn type might spend hours at the ruins of the world's oldest pyramid at Sakkara, while the other types playfully ride camels on the Giza plateau or return exhausted to the hotel to lie by the pool.

To the Saturn type, everything and everyone in the world is either worth their 'attention', or is not. They normally do not like anything or anyone they consider 'silly': parties, dilettantes, gossip conversations, 'fashion' . . . and they loathe the superficial and the pretentious in people, in the arts, in politics.

For Saturn types, everything is a question awaiting an answer. They will feel satisfied only when all has been deconstructed, analysed, cross-referenced and re-integrated in a way that reveals the larger, hidden meaning. They long to understand the mysteries of life, the essence of everything.

This constant intellectual hunger is why Saturn types choose relationships that will give them an opportunity to teach or learn. But more often than not, other types find Saturnine heavy seriousness to be extremely depressing. And indeed, Saturn types themselves often suffer from depression because they realize how hopeless many of the problems of the world are. They rarely indulge in the optimism of wishful thinking, but can sometimes – in the darkest of situations – provide odd relief with unexpected bursts of wit and clown-like behaviour. Their lack of self-consciousness leaves them free to poke fun at themselves or others, particularly if it will serve a worthy purpose.

Saturn types command respect by the quality they bring to their work, and the dignity of their presence. They hold themselves to a high level of performance and demand the same of their subordinates. Their rigorous investigation of the theories and conclusions of others is often intimidating.

Saturn types are seen as 'other' by many people because their quiet, serious nature makes them seem unfriendly and potentially critical. The mental power that shines through their eyes is often so unnerving that people do not notice their most distinctive feature, *something no other type has*: you can look deep into the eyes of a Saturn type and feel as if you could *enter their world*.

The drawbacks of the Saturn type are difficult to list because they overlap with their good qualities: they demand uncompromising excellence from others but also from themselves; they tend toward quiet, non-engaging behaviour which others may mistake for apathy; their seriousness and general sobriety can have a depressing 'kill-joy' effect. And most important: their perfectionism causes them to revise their works-in-progress endlessly rather than complete anything. They are always working on 'too many' projects because of their wide interests.

But if you want a wise mentor, a stable, interesting friend whom will always speak objective truth, even at their own expense, you can do no better than a healthy Saturn type.

Mars Type
Definition: The Athlete–Warrior, Sportsman

The Mars type is the second of the two 'movement' types. Mars actions are direct, unsubtle, blunt and powerful, as compared to the much gentler, much 'busier' Mercury types.

The Mars essence-type energy is characterized by boldness and clarity of purpose. Sports figures and soldiers know their goals and take clear, decisive steps to achieve them. Mars types constantly vie for power and influence, and their strategy often can be described in military or sporting terms: from corporate boardrooms to playgrounds, you hear the Mars-type words 'team', 'on my side', 'win–lose', 'defeat', 'victory'. Sometimes Mars types may present a warm, 'cuddly-bear' appearance, but beneath the smiles and hugs lurks the power of a real bear. Their powerful gestures, their sweeping ambitions, their rousing, charismatic calls to action easily motivate others to join them in pursuit of their goals. They welcome any like-minded allies, and highly value loyalty in others. They can be extremely loyal themselves, and will go to great pains to help their protégés.

A problem arises, however, when anyone criticizes them, since criticism is perceived by the Mars type to be *disloyal*, even when given with the best intentions. Only those extremely close to them, who have proven over time and on many occasions to be wise, loyal friends, dare question them. And, if you urge a Mars type to abandon a course of action, you had better have something powerfully convincing with which to replace their original plan.

Other problems arise from the Mars energy itself, which is the most physically powerful of all the type energies. Mars types thrive on high-stakes competition, and happily test their strengths in the various arenas of life. But 'Mars' is, after all, the Roman god of war, and the powerful Mars energy itself can turn violent when it flows through deranged individuals, of *any* essence type. History is littered with unfortunate examples of Mars energy turned wildly destructive. But for every Hitler, there are many examples of healthy Mars-type energy being used to achieve great works that could only have been done with this energy: the Dwight D. Eisenhower National System of Interstate and Defense Highways was championed by the great general who led the massive war effort which defeated Hitler.

On the less spectacular, individual level, the Mars type is more likely to dominate by excelling as a lead player in whatever 'game', in whatever field of endeavour they choose. Healthy Mars types learn to help rather than to dominate others although there is seldom any question regarding who is holding the reins. In the early stages of a relationship they will test the loyalty of their loved one and hopefully the relationship will not flounder. If the relationship is ending, the Mars type will often feel sincere concern and genuinely try to repair the damage.

A youthful Mars type, in a work situation, will look for a mentor figure to guide them in their efforts, but a Mars type expects no favours. They want to progress by doing the work better than anyone else. An older Mars type, already in a position of power, will seek out protégés, and will hold them to a high standard of performance. And their protégés had better be ready to work long and hard to show their gratitude and worthiness. Once a loyalty connection has been established, the Mars type often proves extraordinarily generous and unselfish. It is not uncommon for Mars types to promote the career of a loyal, capable assistant, even if it means losing them. And, if this happens, the Mars type often watches their progress proudly from afar.

A Mars type comfortably in power will want to help others that he/she thinks are worthy. But a Mars type without power – marooned in a menial position, unemployed, or physically incapacitated, is often curiously helpless because when the 'oversize' plans of Mars types go wrong, they experience an 'oversize' sense of failure. The Mars type then tends to take one of two routes:

1. They may become suddenly, almost irrationally inspired by possibility, and then they can overcome enormous problems, even physical ones.

   or

2. They get depressed and lose all hope. In this latter case, they often want to be left alone, but this is the worst choice possible. An 'intervention' is definitely indicated, since only someone they love and trust can revive their sense of optimism and their will to live.

Mars types often tempt physical disasters because their natural boldness and competitive nature takes them into dangerous situations. They like to climb treacherous mountains, go white-water rafting, and be where dangerous events are taking place, just for the sake of the challenge. And, hopefully, they survive. This seemingly reckless need to test the boundaries of their capabilities has had many positive aspects over the centuries.

What would the world be without Mars energy: without the adventurers who went to the Moon, the Arctic poles, and the depths of the sea; the visionaries who built great civilizations, and the early mariners, the intrepid souls who left sight of land and sailed into the unknown to discover what lay beyond the horizon? And where would we be without the brave Mars leaders who went to battle to restore peace on so many occasions?

But what may be most valuable to us as individuals is the simple personal 'Yes, I can!' energy that the Mars type fosters in all of us. And whatever our essence type, we must learn to use our own Mars-type energy, because this is what we need to accomplish the difficult tasks in our lives.

25

Jupiter type (7)
Definition: The Jolly 'Feeding' Parent, Giver, Peacemaker

To appreciate the characteristics of the Jupiter type it is necessary only to think of the sun: radiant warmth, benevolence, golden generosity, selflessness. Each of these ideas conveys an aspect of the largest of the type-energies.

Jupiter types are the second of the emotional types and they are, by far, the most kind, stable, and predictable of all the types. They are earth-centered, slow to change, and although they do everything in their power to promote happiness wherever they are, they dislike the silly, and the frivolous. They radiate strong loving energy outward into the space around them, as opposed to Venus types (the other emotional type) who seem to pull energy in toward them. Normally the slowest of the essence energies, Jupiter types speak and move slowly, and often with attractive, gentle gracefulness.

Jupiter types tend to like largeness. They enjoy large homes, large clothes wafting around them, and they like large ideas not burdened with too many details. Lovers of relaxation and comfort, their homes are filled with overstuffed furniture and 'friendly' pillows waiting on inviting couches. They are often excellent cooks and need to watch their diet since largeness of body doesn't seem to bother them. And, sometimes unfortunately, they rarely like physical exercise done for its own sake.

Mostly they do not say much, preferring to *listen* as a bene-volent presence. When they talk about someone it will never be to criticise, because they try to understand everyone, and, if necessary, embrace the person's flaws. A typical interchange will involve their being very concerned about you, while totally ignoring their own problems. They are gregarious and like gatherings, especially of friends and family, but, unlike the Mars–Jupiter hybrid type, the pure Jupiter is usually not anxious to have a bold leadership role in society at large.

Of all the other types, only Saturn types understand the pure form of love that results from the Jupiter planetary energy. Jupiter's sister type, Venus, often sees the always-benevolent, unselfish Jupiter types as being false, insincere. But the kind, grandparental nature of Jupiter types is *always sincere*. The Jupiter type, more than any other type, abhors conflicts of any kind and almost compulsively acts as peacemaker on any occasion. If someone has to be the 'fall guy', the loser, the guilty one, they will take the scapegoat role upon themselves, since they have little need for the praise of others, and will find more quiet dignity in taking blame than in giving it. Jupiter types make excellent judges precisely because they are loath to judge others. The important thing to them is preserving or regaining peacefulness in the world around them.

Being innately self-sacrificing, unselfish and long-suffering, Jupiter types are frequently taken advantage of by other types, and everyone is amazed that the Jupiter type doesn't seem to mind. With a smile and the words 'It's all right,' they will forgive almost anything. But this type, normally benign, gentle and forgiving can become fiercely combative if they witness deliberate cruelty directed toward someone who seems 'helpless'. Then, and only then, the Jupiter type becomes aroused to use all the force they have against the perpetrator. (This is most true if the meanness is directed toward children or helpless animals.)

Jupiter types have a unique ability always to regard whoever is in front of them at the moment to be the sole object of their concern. They have infinite patience listening to the problems, hopes and dreams of others, and – especially when young people are involved – they will go out of their way to give them assistance by way of recommendations, introductions and often through anonymous gifts. Jupiter types express genuine fondness of children, and as often happens with doting grandparents, children gravitate to them, trust them, and love them in return. When a child says, 'I love you' to them, the Jupiter breaks into a warm, satisfied smile that is marvellous to see.

When a Jupiter type is alone with others, they remember much that the person has told them on previous occasions and are eager to discuss what is important to the other person. They like to give presents they think the recipient will like; they remember the birthdays of others; and when they travel, they like to bring home little gifts that wlll please the people they know. Often highly intelligent the Jupiter usually feels oddly inadequate academically. They rarely challenge the incorrect 'facts' of others, even if they know them to be inaccurate, because peace and harmony are much more important to them than winning an intellectual contest. They tend to dislike formal study but learn a great deal from what others tell them. 'Sit down and tell me all about it,' is what they frequently say to others who have had interesting adventures.

Jupiter types love to smile and laugh. Their happiness is quite 'infectious', and when a Jupiter type doesn't seem to be brimming with joy, the people close to them become concerned that they are ill. Jupiter types definitely possess the 'best sense of humour' of any of the types. However, their 'humour' often has multiple meanings not immediately evident. Yes, they like to be surrounded by laughter and happiness, and they enjoy creating a 'jovial' atmosphere, or spreading the joy by joining the laughter of others. But the one role they never shirk from is that of the peacemaker, and by laughing, they may actually be smoothing over difficult situations. If they feel the slightest tension in a gathering, Jupiter types often say something amusing, or laugh for no reason at all, and their jolly nature makes everyone feel welcome, wanted, and loved in a way that disperses all potential discord.

Jupiter types choose familiar, comfortable places to go on holiday, or they go to visit someone they know. But if they have a 'cause', they can be unbelievably adventurous and, filled with great dynamism, vigor and optimism, they might go to dangerous, impoverished places where they will work to help alleviate hunger and general misery.

What bothers them on a personal level is what they see as their failure to realize that a friend needed help. They will feel upset that they didn't respond to a hint that someone they know needed a small loan. This 'neglect of a friend' will bother them until they rectify the situation. Jupiter types, despite their jolly nature, take the problems of others seriously, and they can easily become 'heavy', weighted down with various self-imposed burdens that have nothing to do with them personally. And worse, they often suffer over things affecting their friends – things that cannot be changed. This inability to help those close to them can lead the Jupiter type into a type of paralysis where all their thoughts and feelings are devoted to the impossible outcome, and it can seem as if everything in their own life has ground to a virtual standstill.

A major problem that affects the lives of many Jupiter types is that of extravagance. Their instinctive generosity towards others, and their natural love of luxury and 'large living' often makes them spend beyond their means. Friends who warn the Jupiter type of impending financial disaster get only a vague smile of thanks 'but I'm all right'. The Jupiter seems to be in a trance of false optimism, and if they do not awaken to their condition in time, they can lose their homes, their savings, and often their friends who are angered by their acts of (seemingly) wilful self-destruction. If this were happening to anyone else, the Jupiter type would find a way to help, but when it happens to them, they are often totally oblivious to the problem. Sometimes only a serious loss or a powerful intervention by persistent friends will awaken them in time.

The tragic paradox of the Jupiter type is that these generous beings, wanting only the best for everyone and willing to set aside their own needs to help others, can be misunderstood and undervalued by those unappreciative of even suspicious of their genuine love for humanity. We need to value Jupiter types, and make sure they don't 'give too much', because these caring loving people, who rarely ask for anything in return, are unique. These 'great givers' do something no other type does: if we let them, they will lead us to love and cherish ourselves. They will teach us what true love is.

The descriptions above are not exhaustive; they are an introduction to the types, an impression of the principal characteristics, traits and workings of the different energies.

The 12-type Enneagram is distinguished by the remarkably specific nature of the information. For instance, ordinarily it does not matter if we say someone is 'kind' or they are 'warm'. But it does here because being 'kind' is a Lunar-type trait, although Lunar type is too isolated to be warm, while 'warm' is a Venus-type trait, but individuals may be too self-centred to be kind. And if both qualities – 'kind' and 'warm' – occur in the same person, we are probably dealing with a Jupiter type. You may not have fully recognized yourself in the descriptions. You may think, 'I'm that, but I'm *equally* that as well.' Perhaps you are a hybrid type, discussed in the next chapter.

Before we turn our attention to the hybrid types, here are some further aspects of the knowledge contained in the 12-Type Enneagram.

Type Blindness

Being in our own essence energy brings with it a particular blindness. When we are in our essence type we are *not aware* of how deeply and completely we are a Lunar or Mercury or Jupiter type and often we cannot see a solution outside our essence energy. For example, a Mercury type will use only movement, organizing, busy-ness, to solve a problem. A Venus type jilted in love is truly bereft since love not only promises all, but failure in love is annihilation: they can discern no compensation in the pleasures available in other type-energies. A Jupiter type will try offering their generous love and good-will and if it is not successful may turn their disappointment on themselves, rather than recognizing the illogicality of this response. So, even if we are a 'good representative' of our essence type, and we may be distinguished in our field and happy in our relationships, we are still *limited* by it.

Type Limitations and the Solution

Type limitation is not a shortcoming of the system. It is fundamental to the unique wisdom and practical usefulness of the 12-type Enneagram. To begin completing what is missing in your own essence energy, it is necessary to *advance towards the next type*. This is part of the value of the number sequence 1, 4, 2, 8, 5, 7. Wherever you begin, this is the sequence that needs to be followed in order to gain from the following, and then each other, type-energy, so someone beginning in Mercury type (2) would follow the sequence 2, 8, 5, 7, 1, 4, and so on. By following the sequence we discover:

> **Lunar type:** This type often looks for someone to look after them, to fill in the gaps in their self-care. By advancing towards Venus type energy, the Lunar type learns to care for themselves.
> **Venus type:** The still-centred, slow-moving Venus type benefits from advancing towards the faster energy of Mercury type. By advancing, the Venus type speeds up their thinking

and actions and discovers that they are able to complete tasks without relying on others.

Mercury type: Over-committed and unrealistic about the time things take, Mercury types live life on the frantic surface. Instead of relying on speed they need to slow down, discover an inner sense of gravity, learn to think their thoughts through and work for a deeper connection and commitment to themselves. For this they need to go towards Saturn type.

Saturn type: Serious and philosophical, interested in the life of the mind, this type prefers solitude. Moving out of the confines of their mind or their workroom, they benefit from Mars type's directness and boldness.

Mars type: The forever brooding and bubbling, potentially volcanic energy of this type needs a focus and a purpose bigger than their need to control and dominate. By advancing towards the selfless love of humanity evinced by Jupiter type, they find a purpose for their fiery essence energy that is useful and admirable.

Jupiter type: The depth of feeling and love for humanity embodied in this type gets turned inward, leading to grief, despair and self-punishment over what they cannot accomplish. By advancing towards the light, irresponsible and playful energy of Lunar type, the Jupiter type acquires relief and perspective.

Although the brief descriptions make it seem easy, journeys towards the next type are in reality much more complex and more fascinating than this. The 12-type Enneagram categorizes everything from the intense pre-occupation of Lunar type to the universal selflessness of Jupiter type. There is a mathematically elegant precision in its design and it embraces emotion, thought, movement, sensuality, power and fulfilment.

A Simple Depiction of the Type-Energies

What examples can we readily find of the proper sequence of type-energies? What is something simple, everyday, concrete in our lives? Let's look at something we do every morning:

We wake up from *Lunar-type dream sleep.* We take a moment to lie in bed, to gather our thoughts for the day and decide what we are going to wear in *Venus-type energy.* Then we rise briskly, make our bed, shower and clean our teeth in *Mercury-type energy*. At this point the three 'younger' types often cease to progress through the energies, and spend the rest of the day moving from one to the other of these three energies. Advanced, or developed, younger types and the older types will continue to progress through the Enneagram.

So, having arrived at work, if we are of the older types we begin to engage with the day, reading and digesting the newspaper, and thinking about the contents of our 'in' tray in *Saturn type*. Then there are meetings to attend with points to be made plus office-political challenges to be seen off or difficult customers to be dealt with using *Mars-type energy*. By the evening we will be ready to relax, unwind and reflect on what we have accomplished, a satisfying process we will enjoy most in *Jupiter-type energy*.

What about the other six, the hybrid-type energies? It is not so much that there are six more examples of how we use a hybrid energy in getting through the day, more that hybrid types will use a combination of the main-type energies in their daily life – as we will explore in the next chapter.

Chapter 3

Introducing the Six Hybrid Types

If we consider the lines that link in a progressive journey of the numbers – 1, 4, 2, 8, 5, 7 and back to number 1 – hybrid types, at any moment, are *somewhere* on the line between two main-type energies. It is important to understand that the particular influence may change from moment to moment, and that at times the result will be recognizably *one* type rather than the other, while at other times the result will be the combined influence of *both*.

The apparent advantage to being a hybrid is obvious: being equally at home in two centres, the individuals have the ability to exploit the characteristics of both energies profitably. However, the hybrids are 'becoming' types, and they are less 'stable and unchangeable', obviously, since they are between two main type energies. The dual influences can potentially have the effect of 'pulling the person apart' although this would be an unfortunate situation and more often the hybrid types learn to balance, and profit from, their dual influences.

Lunar–Venus Type
Childlike Adult, Sensual, Affectionate, Vulnerable

The dreamy innocence of the eternal child wrapped in the body of a sexually irresistible woman: does that remind you of a famous blonde film star of the 1950s? Marilyn Monroe, both in the movie characters she portrayed, and in her essence, was a Lunar–Venus hybrid type. This type is poised between the *intuitive knowledge* of Lunar type and the *emotional earthiness* of Venus type. Being partway between two types they will have a delightful lightness in their thinking as well as an attitude to sex that is unabashed and refreshing. This is one of the two most vulnerable types since they are moving away from the shrewdness of Lunar type and are not fully grounded in the self-care of Venus type. This type enjoys flirting with disaster, and they often appear to be holding their lives together with not much more than a smile.

They often become sexually experienced before other types, which leads to their being very confident around sex but also to following a behaviour pattern of using sex *for all their feelings of confidence and self-worth*. Their private lives are often over-complicated and under-fulfilling. They have little difficulty in attracting admirers but will treat their partners with indifference, retreating back to Lunar-type dreaminess and abandonment rather than moving forward towards Venus-type sexual/emotional responsibility. They may talk their way into a job (or see nothing wrong with *sleeping* their way up) but their type-energy lacks the resilience and stick-to-it attitude necessary for advancement. Thus they often find their ways into jobs or careers that are freelance, part-time or temporary: actors, waiters, event-catering.

With the 'younger' types such as the Lunar–Venus type, it is helpful to remember that you cannot have an army comprised entirely of generals. We need lesser-ranking men and women. Not everyone wishes to strive for greatness; some just want to have fun and be loved. The Lunar–Venus type likes to mention serious health issues in an off-hand manner but when questioned further they will dismiss the subject with a dazzling, sexy shrug. Underneath they are riddled with insecurity and self-doubt, partly because the influence of these two energies leads to a vulnerable result and partly because the forms of work they pursue tend to offer them little stability or security.

Venus–Mercury Type
The Busy, Fun-Loving Lover

This type's dual influences are *emotion* and *speed*. The result is a warm, supportive, loyal individual who fizzes with activity. When moving house they unpack everything in a blindingly short time. However, because they are driven by a need for *order* rather than *logic*, some of the options they choose will make little sense. They may claim they need to rest (Venus-type influence) but on days off they will fill up the hours meeting friends and other energy-eating activities (Mercury-type influence). This type can cause confusion for their loved ones because they seem to be sensual and devoted to one-to-one times, yet rather than enjoying the quiet of home they are constantly out in the world and a partner must learn that they also prize their friendships, and not force an ultimatum on them.

Where the person is overly influenced by Mercury type they tend towards the flippant and superficial. Consider the hero or heroine of a 'screwball comedy' – they drive their loved ones to distraction by being more interested in making wisecracks than making love. A romantic dinner is an opportunity to send up the waiter (sweetly, they aren't vindictive); they may enjoy pretending to have a coughing fit as their beloved leans in for the clinch. Because they are moving away from Venus type and towards Mercury type, their lovemaking in any case will probably be brisk and less relationship defining. They are great readers and, depending on how advanced the individual is, their choice of material will range from heavily emotional pulp fiction to a spiritual quest, although their interests in spirituality will be more of an expression of emotion than an academic exploration.

They *need* to be popular and even if they are important only to their fellow office workers they take great pride in reporting any positive comments made about them, especially on their being *youthful* (Venus-type happiness) or *multi-talented/tasking* (Mercury-type happiness). One major advantage with this hybrid is that unlike the pure Venus types, who harbour grudges, they tend to forget and move on. This is highly advantageous since it prevents a relationship from descending into a spiral of both sides taking defensive positions. However, this characteristic brings benefits *only if the other side can recognize the advantages of this way of operating.* If the other side sees this type's difficulty in arguing logically as an opportunity to walk over them, this type experiences much unhappiness, which, since they are 'fun-loving', is particularly unfortunate.

Mercury–Saturn Type
The Busy Thinker

Their dual-influence ability to *think* at *speed* nicely aligns this hybrid with the principal demands of modern living. What is often most desirable is quick, informed thinking and, for example, a publisher's eyes light up at a writer who is this hybrid as they can be counted on for one novel (or more) a year. They are sincere in their intellectual pursuits, but since this hybrid type is only somewhere on the path *towards* Saturn their creative output is presented in an entertaining rather than a weighty way and they are not 'deadly serious' like the pure Saturn type.

Being the most developed of the *younger* types they are poised between the maturity and outward-looking attitude of the older types and the inner-directed, personal needs of the younger. Some of their relationship choices may be unwise since they will not have considered the consequences of an unsuitable choice and may take a partner who doesn't fit, for example a needy Lunar type. They are thus forced into an ongoing Saturn/Jupiter-type support role, making it difficult to get support for their own needs.

These hybrids dazzle with their quick wit, leading to early recognition and, typically, fairly easy advancement. Because of the number of areas or tasks covered they may appear to be more capable than they are: when the going gets stressful they may fall back on their *younger* energy and surprise people who thought they would 'handle it better'. This is also why the mature artist of one year can produce a naïve and unsuccessful offering the next. They can be uneasily aware of living on the surface and skimming rather than being properly focused, but unless they are prepared to work on the Saturn-type influence they will lack the ongoing depth of engagement needed to change in a permanent, meaningful way.

We now leave the territory of the 'younger' types and cross The Divide into the territory occupied by the 'older' types. There is information on The Divide in a following chapter.

Saturn–Mars Type
The Socially Active Thinker, The Power-Driven Planner

In this hybrid, the *gravitas* of Saturn type combines with the *fiery need for supremacy* of Mars type. These are social and personal agitators, ambitious and gifted in self-promotion, who want others to join *their* band or party. They have a genius for catching the mood, either of the moment or the country, and examples of this type have included socially active actresses, famous politicians and some of the world's most infamous tyrants. They may not be academically minded, but in order to get the right degree or attention they are capable of turning out impressive dissertations, manifestos and books on their agendas or vision.

They are serious people, with serious goals. They will not remain in the shadows since they sincerely believe their charisma and celebrity are good for business. Here they chime perfectly with the modern mood for secular idolatry. In achieving their vision they will not hesitate to trample on the opposition. They are unenviable opponents because they make use of their encyclopedic knowledge, which would be formidable enough, but they also blithely, relentlessly and mercilessly deny the other's truth, regardless of what they know the truth to be.

Their ability to make things happen often makes them successful, although along the way they will discard all those who don't agree with them. The relentless self-promotion can also backfire because the type is *so* busy self-promoting that they forget that other people have their own story, and their own lives to live, rather than being content with the Saturn–Mars type's appointed role of audience, satellite, colleague, wife or house-husband.

Mars–Jupiter Type
The Humanitarian, Benevolent Forcefulness

This hybrid type is the strongest of all. They are unbelievably tough and resilient. They often need all their might in order to actualize the huge concerns and agendas they bear on behalf of others. Their desire to help is not tempered by a reverence for the status quo and they operate in a way others experience as extremely bossy – 'benevolent *forcefulness*'. They care nothing for their own safety when getting involved in other people's business (like Victorian missionaries, taking it on themselves to bring Christianity to the hostile residents of Africa and Asia) and undertake enormously daunting projects because they genuinely believe their way is better (such as the hospital matron who terrorises the new student nurses into becoming excellent). On a more modest scale the type-energy may manifest in an individual who rejects worthless work because they are adhering to their strict moral code, holding out for work that is meaningful to them and valuable for others.

Personal relationships are not high on this hybrid's list and they may let down a lover, or their children, in order to take a political or social stand with the masses. However, they are aware of the suffering they inadvertently cause, and are sincere in wishing all well – they just know where their priorities have to lie. Although they may not be strong physically, they draw strength from their *ideals* and put across their message quietly but with complete, uncompromising determination. Martyrdom is not sought, but neither is it feared. It is accepted as the potential price of following their inner beliefs.

With hindsight we can see that some of these sincere beliefs may be unfortunate. Missionaries often suffered for their zeal and nowadays we question whether they had the *right* to determine the faith of other peoples. At their best their radiance inspires whole nations yet their unceasing ability to discover causes can be daunting to others. However, the benevolent influence of Jupiter type allows them to take a different tack from the opposition-denying, pure Mars-type energy, because if something *better* comes along, or if they see the sense in going forward in a different way, they are able to drop their previously held belief instantly in favour of a new one that is more suitable.

Jupiter–Lunar Type
The Fairytale Friend, Parent, Child

The final hybrid type combines the essence of the strong, reliable parent with the eternal innocence and vulnerability of the child. This combination makes it hard for others to know if they should *parent* them, or if they should allow the Jupiter–

Lunar type to parent *them*. The answer is that at times both are appropriate and even necessary. Unlike the pure Lunar type this hybrid is not lost in an inner world. Instead, although they fit easily into Lunar type's creative fantasy and are comfortable in a make-believe world, they *have the authority to take charge in it*. They have no problem in believing in the mysterious and the supernatural because they see little distinction between the real and the fantastic and are enthusiastic followers of conventional religions and alternative faiths. They are prized by such organizations because they volunteer for the boring admin jobs others carefully avoid.

This hybrid charms and disarms by their spontaneity – one moment serious, the next shining-eyed and innocently radiant. They may deeply desire to be half of a couple, and dream of having their own children, to whom they can relate both as a parent and a delightful friend. Their competence and work ethic will gain them a position of responsibility but their own needs will be a confusing area, both for themselves and the significant other: this is why they are the other most vulnerable of the types. The Jupiter-type benevolence causes them to step aside in favour of any other candidates, and even if they try they cannot avoid making a chum out of a potential mate. What they have going for them is that their complex inner world makes them able to empathize with just about any situation, so drawbacks other types would find deal-breaking they willingly, even eagerly embrace. ('Widower with three kids – I'm there!')

Benevolent to the point of naivety, they are often deeply upset and disappointed by the wickedness or selfishness of the world. Being under the influence of the largeness of Jupiter, they find a way to accept such disillusionment without abandoning their optimistic view of people. Their desire to avoid hurting others may also mean that bad temper or any letting off of steam will be done in private, and taken upon themselves ('You really aren't as wonderful as they think you are!' to their mirror). They often gravitate into jobs in the caring or charity sector where, if they do not recognize their own needs, they may take on the desperate plight of others and suffer for what they cannot make right. Usually, however, the strength of Jupiter type protects the vulnerability of Lunar type, giving us a delightful companion or work colleague who is both highly competent and also spontaneously funny to be around.

How Should the Hybrid Types Develop?

Each main type's most desirable path of development is to move in the direction of the next main-type energy. How does this apply for the hybrid types? For some, the next type-energy would be more of a halfway house and their most desirable path of development would be the main-type energy after that:

> **Lunar–Venus type:** An element of Venus-type energy is scrupulousness in sexual matters. For this hybrid, with its exciting and chaotic libido, it is enough to work towards securing the stabilizing influence of Venus-type energy.
>
> **Venus–Mercury type:** This hybrid tends to know how to do things at a faster rate. There is always benefit in doing this more consciously, but the true path of development for the Venus–Mercury type is accessing deeper-thinking, characteristic of Saturn type.
>
> **Mercury–Saturn type:** Because so much of the world operates in quasi-Mercury-type speed and superficiality, which exacerbates this hybrid's freneticism, it is enough for this hybrid to work towards manifesting the deep seriousness of Saturn type.
>
> **Saturn–Mars type:** The most desirable path of development for this hybrid is to employ the seriousness of Saturn type and the drive of Mars type in moving towards the ultimate destination, the conscious manifestation of Jupiter type.
>
> **Mars–Jupiter type:** This magnificent hybrid gains both from the satisfied rest of Jupiter type and the lightness of Lunar type.
>
> **Jupiter–Lunar type:** Having the dual influences of parent and childlike adult and feeling confused in sexual relationships, this hybrid's final destination is to work towards the emotional maturity of a developed Venus type.

These descriptions, and those for the six main types, focus on the most immediate path of development. There is a greater adventure, the journey by which each type visits each of the other types, in the correct order, to learn how to manifest their characteristics. We will examine this process later in the book.

Different Type Realities

Every person, each *essence type*, has their own sense of reality. Every essence type has *their own version* of reality, their own evaluation of what is important in their life, and their distinctive area of deep concern. What is 'reality' and what is 'important' differs from type to type. This does not need to be corrected and reduced into a single, universally applicable standard or mode of operating. In fact, this has been a basic problem: because the existence of the 12 different essence types has not been general knowledge, *the understandings, allowances and support for the differences in types have gone unrecognized and been entirely ignored.*

We need to be aware that most people, when first reading information about types, imagine that they are many types, every type, or the one type that is their *fantasy* type, which does not describe the reality of who they actually are. Everyone around them probably knows they are not what they try to be, or think they are. Those around them might be able to see that they would be much more comfortable, much happier, living a different way, *in a different type*. Everyone around them *knows*, and can see these things . . . except the person involved.

We all say 'I am what I am and I can't change it' and we think that makes us strong, when those around us can see it makes us weak. In truth, we have the ability to change, to modify, and to gain for ourselves all that would make us truly strong, creative and flexible to face life's challenges: *we need to go consciously to the appropriate type-energy.* However, up till now, this process, this knowledge, this *system* was not available to us.

Where Do We Go Now?

Up to this point, the emphasis has been on distinguishing and identifying the different essence energies. Yet we will never encounter someone who is entirely *one* essence energy, since we have, in different concentrations, all 12. A proper understanding and use of the 12 would be highly desirable, yet the reality of all our lives is that we are most often unconsciously *operating out of type.* We need more information to break down and then rebuild our present less desirable and even harmful practices. There are elements that enhance and complicate type-energies such as *type defaults* and *split types*. We will learn that there are special relationships between particular pairs of types in the form of *shared functions* and *dominant centres*. In communicating there are *different understandings of the same word*, and later we will examine how each type lives, works, loves and relaxes in its own, specific, way. We must consider the influence of the triangle 3, 6, 9. As well, there is *The Divide* and each type's *Higherself.* So there is a great deal to be getting on with as we continue to explore the fascinating 12-type Enneagram.

Chapter 4

Elaborating on the Types

Unconsciously Manifesting the Different Types

So far the emphasis has been on separating and identifying the traits of the 12 type-energies. Since we have all the types inside us, we are in constant, unconscious, undirected movement around the Enneagram. We can think of ourselves as having the building blocks for *12 different personalities*. As we read this, remember that we will only have one essence type, so where the other type-energies are noted, these will be our essence type's *interpretation* of the other energies.

For example, we are in a good mood, quite playful and friendly (Lunar type). We see on the other side of the road an acquaintance and we wave but they don't acknowledge this; in fact they seem to ignore us, which makes us hostile (Mars type). We examine our mental files to determine why they have ignored us (Saturn type) but then decide to give them the benefit of the doubt (Jupiter type). We then pass a stranger who we find physically attractive (Venus type) and rush round the block to encounter them again (Mercury type).

Let's continue with reference to the hybrid types. We stop to talk and flirt with the attractive stranger (Lunar–Venus type). They respond to our breezy fun-loving attitude (Venus–Mercury type) and we snap off some witty observations (Mercury–Saturn type). Then they speak, and we are shocked by an off-hand, racist comment we need to challenge (Mars–Jupiter type). They respond positively to our clear directive (Saturn–Mars type) and we make a date to meet again. But then we have doubts as to their sincerity and decide not to put ourselves in a potentially compromising situation (Jupiter–Lunar type).

This illustration gives us a taste of the reality of how we perpetually bounce unconsciously, from one type-energy to the next. It is random. But there are a number of type functions that are *not* random, that are 'law-conformable' within the system.

Type-Defaults

In a sense, *everything* is concerned with 'type-defaults'. Every moment during which an individual functions in their own essence type they are also *defaulting unconsciously* to their type. Something to remember here is that often *everyone else* can see this – except the person whose type is involved in the observation. For example, a Mercury-type office worker will burn up the carpet running to and fro but if she is asked to slow down she will be bewildered: she won't have seen how she operates differently from others – 'but I'm only doing what everyone else does'. Therefore, 'type training' begins with seeing *your own defaults*, but going much deeper than you usually do – seeing your essence type-energy default *objectively* as well as *subjectively*. 'People used to make me feel guilty because I like to lie around the house at the weekend. Now that I know I'm a Venus type, I know this is me manifesting my essence energy. But now I also know when I've had enough and then I whiz around in Mercury energy, cleaning the flat.'

Aside from the default into the essence type, we more often default into *our type* version of other type-energies. There are two categories here. Firstly the ongoing, unconscious, bouncing round the Enneagram, responding to whatever stimulus we receive from the outer world. The second category is the 'law-conformable' operation of the Enneagram, with specific type-energies to which each type will default. A simple definition of 'default' here is that it is the type of energy to which the named type will *go under duress*, when they are overtired, or when they do not have the energy to maintain their own type. It is not just a 'quirk' or 'blip': there are meaningful reasons why a particular type defaults to another type.

> **Lunar type:** Lunar type defaults to *Mars type*. This might at first appear the most surprising default. For the gentle energy of Lunar type to be full of the fierce energy of Mars type – with the predictable combustion – seems a strange

state of affairs in what is essentially a system aiming towards balance, support and completeness. However, if we consider that the Lunar type is the most *vulnerable* type, it becomes a feature which can help enormously: if there is not any other way by which the Lunar type can find protection, *the Lunar type contains the means for its own protection and survival.* This is why children who have suffered abuse develop hard shells.

For the Lunar type, defaulting into Mars type is a mixed blessing. While in Mars type they may do themselves damage, because observers may believe they have seen the 'real person' rather than the temporary default. This is true for all types operating out of type.

Venus type: A Venus type, in a tight corner, may default back to Lunar type, adopting a childlike persona, a 'don't blame me, I'm only a ditzy blonde' device for avoiding responsibility or defusing anger. They can also default to bombastic Mars type, which is why hapless husbands, returning home late and inebriated to ordinarily submissive wives, suddenly find themselves on the receiving end of a righteous whirlwind.

Mercury type: Mercury type also defaults into Lunar type. Faced with a problem, the Mercury type *avoids being serious* by distracting themselves. When what is needed is a confrontation, they instead pursue a number of other issues, thus using busy-ness as an excuse for not taking action. Mercury type may also default to Mars type, which may manifest as furious indignation, physical shaking and half-completed, virtually incoherent, threats.

Saturn type: Saturn type defaults into Lunar type. This can be charming, as in those moments when the type's unexpected clumsiness surprises their friends. However, a senior don blocking a junior's advancement because they have taken a dislike to the colour of their car, or their wearing of bow ties, is an example of Saturn type negatively defaulting to Luna. This type can also default to Mars type and become 'deadly serious', ignoring a more benevolent Jupiter-type understanding of another's mistake and instead grinding down the other with merciless, point-scoring scorn.

Mars type: Mars type defaults to Lunar type. This is again surprising, since Mars type *hates* Lunar type's spontaneous, creative behaviour. Lunar type invites other types to join in their magical creation of the world, and Mars type reacts violently against being drawn into anyone else's set of rules. The default may result in a normally formidable person insisting they 'be allowed my little bit of fun'. An unwary Lunar type, lulled into revealing their inner child by seeing their Mars-type boss 'messing around', will join in and feel foolish or tricked when the Mars type suddenly reverts and reasserts control. The default has more serious consequences. A Mars type who acts in an irresponsible way *when they have responsibility* is highly dangerous as in the case of the general who sends his soldiers to their deaths because he is trying to make a point about strategy to another general.

Jupiter type: Jupiter type defaults to Mercury type and runs around trying to save the world by teatime, losing perspective and becoming overwhelmed by impossibility. They can also default to a variety of negative Venus type. When the Venus type becomes negative about their *appearance*, they may go in the opposite direction and insist they are the ugliest person alive. When the Jupiter type becomes negative about their *sense of worth* they think of themselves as useless, unworthy of living.

Hybrid types need to be aware that they will default to the default position of one of their type influences.

Operating out of Type

We have understood that our 'essence type' is defined as that energy we most embody. Each type has its own recognizable characteristics, and some of these are more necessary and suitable for the busy lives we all live than others. Operating out of type is partly a practical matter in that our energy type may be, for example, slower than that required in our job, so we *have to* default. It can also be the result of not having our essence energy understood by others, for example when parents (who may be Saturn or Mars types) force their Lunar- or Venus-type children to follow the parents' choice of career. The Lunar- or Venus-type may attempt to be a lawyer, a doctor or an architect, and develop an attitude to their work as being 'something I do that has nothing to do with me'. This is also an indication of the potential long-term negative effects of operating out of type; at some point the person may rebel, or have a financial or mental/emotional breakdown because they are living so far from their essence energy.

As was noted earlier, because up till now we have not had the information on identifying and consciously manifesting our essence type-energy, we may all find ourselves operating out of type:

- A woman comments that her new boyfriend appears to be a Venus type: he is well groomed, languid and sensuous. So she gives him expensive aftershave and is dismayed when he doesn't wear it. She invites him to art galleries and is confused when he expresses no interest in the paintings but is highly interested in some aspect of the temperature-maintenance controls. She comes to realize that he is in fact a Saturn type, who at some point has worked out intellectually that life would be easier if he operated in Venus type.

- An amateur academic spends many years on a writing project but when he finally shows it to the outside world it is a bewildering mixture of other people's opinions and a child's fantasy: he is a Lunar type operating in his own personal rendition of 'profound thinking', which is not successful because it is not rooted in true Saturn-type depth.

- A woman tells her friends that she passionately supports a cause but in fact she never finds the time to make any meaningful contribution to it. She would believe herself to be a Mars–Jupiter type, but is rather a Mercury type.

- A man with genuine writing talent becomes the creative director of an advertising agency. This position requires Mars-type management skills and because of the fine creative work he produces, the bosses believe he will be competent in the new role. However, the man is a Mercury type and in a management role he focuses on speed rather than depth, resulting in generic work. In confrontation he spins half-digested thoughts that confuse his listeners.

- A woman seeks to disguise the ruthlessness of her Mars-type personality by operating in Lunar type. Unfortunately, the clumsy and blunt manner of her essence type leads to her imagining herself to be witty when actually her aggressive, self-aggrandizing humour rubs people up the wrong way.

- An executive gets jobs by being seemingly perfect. In fact he is a Venus type who has learned to put on a brave show in interviews. But when it comes to delivery, relying on the slower Venus-type energy rather than the multi-tasking Mercury-type energy necessitates his constructing elaborate excuses to hide his shortcomings (his mother has died at least five times).

As these examples illustrate, operating out of type invariably has some sort of consequence, which can range from the minor up to major. The long-term consequences of acting out of type, as noted in Chapter 1, can mean marriages or relationships going wrong, failed careers and mental or emotional breakdowns, heart attacks and even suicide. By now you may be wondering why it is that, since a lack of information on our types can have such a disastrous result, the information is not given to us, ideally while we are growing up. We cannot explain this oversight: all we can do is use the information that is now being offered.

You will have noticed that most types default to Lunar type. This does make logical sense since we have all experienced childhood, we have all experienced feeling weak and helpless, and so, in vulnerable moments, it is to Lunar type that we default. We can learn to observe ourselves more objectively, so that if we are conscious of having defaulted to a different essence energy, we can employ this to our advantage.

As is the case throughout this book, these brief descriptions do not comprehensively convey the many levels and great subtlety involved in this issue. Take these descriptions as a starting point; it is only through personal reflection and observation that these words and concepts will rise from the page and into your consciousness.

Split Types

It is possible that a person can *manifest in equal measure* the essence of two *dissimilar* types (as opposed to hybrid types). Often, though, the person merely wishes to be something they are not. Mercury types often say they are all the types, or that they are anything other than Mercury type. Someone who is actually a Venus type may feel it more desirable to present themselves as a Saturn type, for example someone who always wears black and sits in fashionable cafes drinking coffee and reading Spinoza or Proust. Just do not ask them to explain any complicated philosophical concept because they cannot. A true split type is different; it is akin to someone who is genuinely ambidextrous. Look and see if there are any examples of true split types in your circle. Split types can be opposites, or they can be linked to the three specific beneficial-relationship couples into which the six types fall, as explained below.

Shared Functions and Dominant Centres

Although we have either a main, or a hybrid, essence type, we also have another specific essence type with which we have a special relationship.

These are as follows:

> Lunar and Saturn – intellectual types
> Venus and Jupiter – emotional types
> Mercury and Mars – moving types

(Lunar (1) and Saturn (8)

The dominant centre and shared function here is intellectual. Saturn and Lunar types both use the intellectual centre/ function as their primary way of seeing the world and gaining meaningful information:

- A Lunar type often has flashes of more valuable insight than Saturn type, but Lunar type sees superficially, through the type's undeveloped self-referential orientation of 'everything pertains to me'.
- Saturn types can help Lunar types understand everything, once they can get the Lunar type away from their 'smallness', whereby they filter the whole world through its meaning, or the lack of it, for them personally.
- Lunar type can open the Saturn type's mind to a whole new world, which the Saturn type will then investigate. But without the question being posed by Lunar type, Saturn type might never think of it.

Thus such individuals should strive to originate their creative and other thinking in Lunar type, and then immediately develop it in Saturn type.

Venus (4) and Jupiter (7)

The dominant centre and shared function here is emotion. Venus type sees the world emotionally as one-to-one, and Jupiter type in terms of the universal picture and application:

- The Venus-type energy, being on the right/personal side of The Divide, creates and is most comfortable with one-to-one relationships. Friends are seen on a single basis and may never be introduced to each other.
- Jupiter types are the opposite. Social situations revolve around friends, hospitality, sharing.
- Venus types are highly concerned with status and being 'proper'. Jupiter types are the opposite; they welcome all people, especially encourage those who are needy, do not consider themselves but only the other side.
- Venus types want the same for others that they want for themselves: pampering, comfort, special attention. Jupiter types are not bothered about their own comfort but want to heal, protect and nurture others

Mercury (4) and Mars (5)

The dominant centre and shared function is moving. These two types express life through movement. They operate at the fastest speeds and will use physical action, rather than thinking or feeling, to act and react to life:

- Mercury-type energy is organizational, the busy p.a. or individual who needs to multi-task in a hurry. Mars-type energy is managing and controlling, so the Mars type values the Mercury for organising their paper work and the Mercury type basks in being acknowledged as 'invaluable'.
- Mercury type can be too light and 'airy' whereas Mars type is earthy, so they will add the missing depth to Mercury type.

- Mars type does not like too much detail, they paint with broad brushstrokes and need Mercury type to keep everything working smoothly.
- Mercury types, being on the 'lighter' side, know their management limitations and admire Mars type's boldness and certainty. Mars types highly value loyalty, which they get from Mercury types.

Less Beneficial Effects of Shared Functions

Lunar and Saturn

A Lunar type may not appreciate that they do not have the depth of Saturn-type thinking on an ongoing basis. An example is the Lunar type who, because he/she occasionally verbalizes a profound insight, takes on or is given a role which requires ongoing Saturn-type thinking. Using Lunar-type *imagination* and *self-reference* may cause them to spiral further and further away from what is helpful.

A Saturn type may joke and put themselves down but then be offended by being sidelined or dismissed due to the subsequent loss of respect from others.

Venus and Jupiter

Venus types can become confused about 'love'. They may attempt to spread their natural one-to-one warmth in a wider/ universal form and their essence energy is just not as deep and robust as Jupiter type.

Jupiter types tend, when they encounter internal and external resistance, to take it in on themselves. Someone who attempts to love everyone except themselves will be miserable.

Mercury and Mars

Because Mercury is diametrically opposite Jupiter type they have some of Jupiter type's concern towards others. This leads them to take on an inappropriate number of tasks and volunteer their services in too many directions. Since they are, although the most developed, still on the 'light' or 'younger' side of The Divide they may become overwhelmed and resentful of others' 'incessant' demands.

Mars type's fast operating style means they have an immediate comeback but this is not always a good thing since the type speaks and acts without thinking or considering the effects (for example emotional) on others.

In summary, it becomes clear that there are both positive and negative aspects to the three type-couple beneficial relationships. Becoming aware of the 12-type Enneagram allows us to take advantage of the ease with which we can access the other type's energy, while bearing in mind the potential disadvantages of acting *out of* one's own type-energy. We must also remember that we have *all the types in us*, so we will benefit if we refine and widen our type vocabulary.

Type Pole Influences

Once we have become accustomed to recognizing essence types, we are intrigued by new questions. For example, someone who is a Venus–Mercury hybrid is also capable of outstanding performance in tasks better suited to Saturn types. This could be dismissed as 'well, we know we have all the type-energies' but that seems an inadequate answer. The answer lies in *type pole influences*. These are:

Venus–Saturn

Lunar–Mars

Mercury–Jupiter

It is clearly desirable for the thinking person to be able to function with more facility in their emotions, and vice versa. Type limitations and type blindness may cause both to accept they 'cannot' function in the polar opposite, yet this is not so. In the case of the Venus–Mercury hybrid, moving towards Mercury gives them the energy to continue their journey, and cross The Divide towards Saturn-type energy. It should be noted that the person does not remain here, and in the midst of performing in Saturn-type depth they will again surprise by instantly returning to negative Venus-type emotional neediness. Yet it shows us that we are all capable of accessing our polar opposite.

For the Saturn type, having access to people who embody Venus-type energy is highly desirable. Often the best way to learn is to see it demonstrated and the aware Saturn type will seek out Venus types so they can observe for themselves the manifestations of the different Venus-type energy.

Lunar–Mars

We have already noted how these two types default to each other. Here we consider the same fact in terms of the *benefits*. It is not always negative or inappropriate. The more the types are properly grounded in their own energy, the more they can be free to explore the polar opposite without being unconsciously lost in it. Mars type's ability to charm with genuine, light-hearted humour (rather than heavy, self-aggrandizing efforts) is an example of their gaining from the polar influence of Lunar type. For Lunar type, being able to access Mars-type fiery energy allows them to defend themselves where necessary without burning up from being constantly on their guard.

Jupiter–Mercury

These two types embody speed or the lack of it, which is obviously why they are polar opposites. However, it has already been noted that these types enjoy a special, beneficial relationship so here we see that being polar opposites can be immediately helpful.

Same Centre-Type Forces

The last set of pairs acknowledges the similarities between types in terms of their principal orientation.

Mercury–Mars

Both are concerned with *doing*. Mercury type with the organization of doing, and Mars type with achieving control and dominance through doing.

Venus–Jupiter

Both are motivated by *love*. Venus type by one-to-one love and Jupiter type by love of the whole.

Lunar–Saturn

Both are concerned with *thought*, Lunar type in instant, intuitive answers, and Saturn type in philosophical, profound questioning.

Different Understandings of the Same Word

We assume that everyone who speaks the same language has the same understanding of its ideas and concepts. It is fascinating, and perhaps intimidating, to realize that each type actually understands *differently*. In a later chapter we will explore this idea in more depth, but as a taster, let us consider the concepts of 'Humour' and 'Seriousness' as they pertain to each type.

Humour by type

Lunar: Perky, impish comments: given encouragement these may become bizarre personal narratives.

Lunar–Venus: Innocently suggestive *double entendres*.

Venus: Wry, possibly critical or with a put-down, a slap which turns into a caress.

Venus–Mercury: Humour is incorporated into most things they do.

Mercury: Machine-gun spray, usually half-formed. Often put themselves down.

Mercury–Saturn: Speed and knowledge equals an informed quip.

Saturn: Humour may be lost on other types because it is amusing only if you know the obscure source reference. Unbends with toilet humour.

Saturn–Mars: Wry put-downs based on knowledge of other.

Mars: Crude, simplistic, direct.

Mars–Jupiter: Humour emerges from a worthwhile or important observation.

Jupiter: Jolly, effortless laughter at the simplest things, particularly to contain the moment and support the other/s involved.

Jupiter–Lunar: Fun comes from inside. Their dual influences make them at home with adults and children, and they see the joy and laughter in both.

Seriousness by type

Lunar: Serious about their individuality. Wear clothes to express this but resent being called 'kooky'; are offended when people laugh rather than understand their serious purpose in expressing their uniqueness.

Lunar–Venus: They believe that people don't understand their complexity and see only their external image when they really want to be understood and seen exactly as they are.

Venus: Serious about their feelings, their clothes and their love interests.

Venus–Mercury: Serious about maintaining friendships.

Mercury: Serious about knowing things: the best restaurants, the source for unusual household items.

Mercury–Saturn: Serious about achieving a considerable body of work; quantity may triumph over quality.

Saturn: Serious about issues, ideas, philosophies and religious doctrine/spiritual ideologies.

Saturn–Mars: Serious about social issues and particularly effecting change, with themselves as the centre.

Mars: Serious about position and influence. Serious about performance and loyalty.

Mars–Jupiter: Serious about forcing change, even at their own expense.

Jupiter: Serious about nourishing people and expressing goodness.

Jupiter–Lunar: Serious about responsibility towards others, particularly being a true, loyal friend.

Type Stages

There are three stages of development of any type:

Beginning stage: a 'young' (or undeveloped) example of whatever type, in whom the most valuable traits of the type have not been mastered or absorbed yet. But everything is 'fresh' to them.

Mid-stage: the characteristics are there in their full form but the person may not know quite how to use them wisely; they may still be 'fighting' against their type-nature.

End-stage: a certain type of 'wisdom' enters the picture with each type and they use their 'typetools' efficiently because they understand from experience what their nature does best. This is what we would call a 'developed' type. At this stage, every type – except Mercury – is settled in their type. They cannot even imagine leaving it, and they certainly have no idea how they could possibly function in the next type (this is *type blindness*).

The Special Case of Mercury type

Mercury is the one type that *has* to reach out to the next type, because the incessant super-fast movement of Mercury type takes hold in all three life-function centres (intellectual, emotional and physical movement) and begins to affect them in a negative way: they realize they are moving too fast and they become aware of their own nervousness. They realize that they are deficient in emotional function because emotion needs time to breathe. They also realize that, despite their endless gathering of information, they don't 'know' anything.

This all comes from a type of 'wisdom' – that only hits most types in old age, if at all. Only then do they realize what they have missed, and *feel an intense need* for a *teacher*. However, throughout their life Mercury types feel an intense desire to understand the depth of Saturn-type knowledge and often reach out to one thing after another. When they find things that could make them deeper they revere them but cannot always go where they know they want to go. This is, for instance, the opposite of Lunar types, who do not understand how superficial their entire being can be. But the Lunar types will keep looking and are not burdened by the advanced (or developed) Mercury type's sudden depression when they realise how little they *actually* know. Mercury types collect a lot of information and think they 'understand' the way a Lunar or Saturn type would. An example here is the Mercury type with a fine art degree dragging two children through a museum, yanking them away from each painting as soon as he has finished his dry, factual recitation.

Chapter 5

Further Fundamentals and What Type Are You?

Different Type Speeds

Within the wisdom of the 12-type Enneagram there is a particular phenomenon that enables us to determine which type we are in at any given moment. We can also use this with other people. Be aware that the type identified may be true *only* for the moment so it is best to make a number of observations before determining someone's essence type. The phenomenon that makes type identification easier is that we need only to listen to ourselves or others speak, because *each type speaks at a different, specific speed*. There exists a tape of Sigmund Freud talking at exactly 80 beats a minute. This is the speed at which Saturn types talk, and we can readily see that Freud was indeed the Philosopher–Creator type.

However, this is not the only information type-speed gives us. The speed that people talk also indicates *the speed at which they operate*. This is why the book has alluded to types being 'slower' or 'faster'. When we are in one of these types, we will also function and speak at this speed, *regardless of our actual essence type*, although we will most probably not be as good at manifesting the type characteristics. In other words we might achieve a pseudo-Mercury-type functioning rather than truly developed Mercury-type organization.

The concept that different people talk (and think and operate) at *different and specific speeds* is one of the many features unique to the 12-type Enneagram. It is also one of the many ways in which we can be satisfied that the system is not theory, but absolute, verifiable fact. Here are the specific speeds:

Lunar type:	96 beats per minute
Venus type:	72 beats per minute
Mercury type:	144 beats per minute
Saturn type:	80 beats per minute
Mars type:	120 beats per minute
Jupiter type:	60 beats per minute

The hybrid types do not have six further type speeds. They will operate in one of the six above.

Let us consider some of the ramifications of these differences. A faster type will simply not understand why it takes another type longer to react. It is necessary with Venus and Jupiter types for the other types to make allowance for the slower rate at which they operate and respond. It does not help for a faster-operating Mars type to shout at a Venus type: given more time, the Venus type will be able to demonstrate that they *have* understood.

What effort is involved in the process of moving towards the next type?

Lunar type: It is fairly straightforward for the 96-beat Lunar type to slow down to the 72-beat Venus type. But *will* they? Lunar types often access the speed of Mercury instead, which blunts and coarsens their intuitive ability, and the faster speed tires them out prematurely.

Venus type: For the 72-beat type to move to Mercury involves doubling their operating speed, from 72 to 144.

Mercury type: The speedy Mercury at 144 needs to slow down to 80 to access Saturn-type thinking. This often occurs by sheer exhaustion or, if they are with someone who has knowledge of the 12-type Enneagram, that person (using Saturn-type wisdom and Jupiter-type compassion) can persuade them to slow down.

Saturn type: For Saturn type at 80 beats to move forward to Mars type means speeding up 50 per cent, from 80 to 120 beats. This process involves coming up, at least temporarily, from their deep-rooted introspection and out into the external world.

Mars type: For the bold energy Mars type (120 beats) to go forward beneficially to Jupiter type (60 beats) is, again, a major effort of understanding and will. The Mars type is helped by gaining temporary relief in their demanding life; the resulting calm and feelings of good-will encourages the Mars type to want to continue to experience the rewards of slowing down.

Jupiter type: In order to access the light-thinking and freedom from responsibility of Lunar type, the Jupiter type needs to go from 60 beats to 96 beats: the faster speed gives them less time for inner reflection and conflict.

A Brief Word About Numbers 3, 6 and 9

We will address the triangle in more detail later. For the present, the energy of number '3' is available in order for Venus type (4) to progress towards Mercury type (2) – 72 beats to 144 beats – and the energy of number '6' supports Mars type (5) to progress towards Jupiter type (7). We note that number '3', being on the younger side, is concerned with the personal (as is Venus type) while number '6', being on the older side, is concerned with the outward-looking. The number '9' is also not a type; instead it marks the fulfilment of a cycle round the 12-type Enneagram (after '9' we start again with '1').

Metronome Exercise

A battery-operated metronome or downloaded app., used by singers and musicians, can be used to illustrate the differences in type speeds. Set the device to the specific type speeds and see what happens:

- Trying to talk at 144 beats (Mercury type) will be markedly different from talking at 80 (Saturn type) or 60 (Jupiter type).
- Watch a TV programme, say the evening news, switching your speeds. At 60 beats you will be more concerned with the people who are suffering; at 120 beats you will identify with the power used in quelling civil discord.
- Switching to 72 beats (Venus type) you will become aware of colours and feelings, switching to 96 beats (Lunar type) you may become bored quickly and want to find something more entertaining.

Reading a newspaper in various, conscious, type speeds will also give you insight into how other people, as well as yourself, normally interpret information.

Obviously, using the metronome speeds as a 'party trick' will result in debasing the precious gift of the knowledge contained in the 12-type Enneagram. Therefore always use the exercise respectfully, both towards the person being tested and the very serious intentions of the 12-type Enneagram.

Further Notes on Different Speeds

Undeveloped Lunar types think extremely superficially because they have already made up their minds. Important issues may be decided on a whim or a piece of irrelevant information that crosses their path at the crucial moment. The 96-beat speed incorporates neither the wisdom of Saturn type nor the self-care of Venus type. It is too fast to take others into account (Jupiter type) but not fast enough to self-protect through argument-mastery (Mars type).

Slower Venus type operates from the feeling of something, dreaming it into a thought.

Mercury and Mars types believe the most important thing is to do something. Mercury type will focus on organization; Mars will seek to achieve dominance. Both habitually take little time to think about the outcome, even though both types think rapidly.

Saturn and Jupiter types move, think and feel more slowly because they do everything more deeply. No other type understands why Jupiter type takes so long to 'get going'. The reason is that Jupiter types have many inner conflicts that less deep types do not.

Moving Correctly Round the Enneagram

We have already noted the correct sequence of development of numbers 1, 4, 2, 8, 5, 7, and how each type goes forward to overcome type limitations. In order to bring about a greater sense of inner unity, and to bring the different energies into a more helpful balance, we can also think of movement around the Enneagram as a series of *corrective procedures*:

Lunar type: Constantly thinking, but in a fractured, child-like manner, creates an inner instability and mental speculation which prevents concentration on 'real life' – or even seeing real life – which is necessary for the type in order to be able to express real feeling. Of course Lunar types think they have 'real feeling' because they don't realize that their endless moving thoughts aren't feelings. Thus Lunar type needs to go to Venus type in order to learn about feelings.

Venus type: This type is much more stable in practical ways (being one of the two 'earth-bound', practical types), but the emotions *move constantly*. This keeps Venus types from realizing inner emotional stability and they never see the reality of life as about anything other than 'feeling'. Thus Venus types need to go towards Mercury-type energy in order to open out.

Mercury type: Whole civilizations – the US, the UK and most of the world – go to Mercury-type energy *neurotically*. This is not true Mercury type, which is constant physical motion, not slowed down or hampered by deep feelings or the desire for them. Unfortunately, this type-energy is also not hampered by deep thoughts or self-realization – this type needs to slow down: thus they need to go forwards to Saturn-type energy in order to slow down and experience life on a deeper, more meaningful level.

Saturn type: This type is sometimes concerned with a fruitless search for balance in thought, feeling and movement. Instead of balance, Saturn types often confuse themselves with thinking of too many options (and not doing any of them), going so deeply into thought and emotion that they become confused about limiting their goals, and this brings them to a halt. Thus they need to access Mars-type energy for decision-making and boldness.

Mars type: Wants to 'move' – to get things done, and they have a curious property of not being able to think and act at the same time. This type also needs deeper thoughts and feelings, but usually settles on one thing and believes that following that to a conclusion is all that's necessary (so they will get the job done, but may not consider the feelings of the workers). Thus they need to go towards Jupiter type to grasp the full picture.

Jupiter type: The slowest-operating energy. This type plunges into a world of 'non-movement', a world of great depth of feeling. This can result in enormous internal suffering without any external benefit. Thus this type needs to go towards Lunar-type energy for lightness and the pleasure of not being responsible all the time.

The lines of the Enneagram connect two energy-entities. This is a line coming from ... *and* going to. This is why we must *travel in the right direction* – 1, 4, 2, 8, 5, 7 and back to 1. For example, Saturn type and Mars type are connected by a line. But if Mars type goes backward to Saturn type and tries to be intellectual in a profound way, it may not work because the Mars type will speak from their concept of 'deep seriousness' and become furious when this is not respected. Both energy-entities are compromised. Another example is of Jupiter type swept up in too ambitious an idea coming from Mars type (wrong direction again) and shaken out of Jupiter-type usefulness into a sense of futility and helplessness.

Interpreting 3, 6 and 9

As previously noted, 3, 6 and 9 do not appear in the sequence of numbers 1, 4, 2, 8, 5, 7 because *they are not types*. They form a separate triangle that is related to, and intersects with, the type sequence. Erroneously creating nine types rather than six goes against nature's plan because the sequence 3, 6, 9 has been *deliberately* left out of the 'magic' series of the six types. An interpretation of nine types robs the diagram of its ability to *predict the near future* by seeing the cross-currents of the Innerself, the Outerworld, and the Higherself, at whatever stage we as individuals (whether 'undeveloped' or 'developed'/a 'good representative') have reached in our lives.

What do we mean by 'predicting the near future' and 'the cross-currents'? The energies present in the six types, together with the beneficial forces in 3, 6 and 9, have a constant influence on our lives. We can 'predict' the near future by assessing where we are, by understanding what we have to learn to manifest in ourselves, and by *acting in a way that brings about our goal*. We read about how certain people seem to be able to 'manufacture' good luck, or how they have found 'the pot of gold'; we wonder why we can't be similarly lucky. What is more likely is that *the right kind of effort* has brought about their success: *success is a process* and by having a more objective sense of what is necessary, we help ourselves to be helped by internal and external forces. We also take advantage of our type characteristics and consciously avoid being misled or blind-sided by our type limitations.

The 3, 6, 9 Triangle

The numbers 3, 6 and 9 form a separate cosmic symbol that clearly involves cosmic force movement *around the triangle itself*, and this movement does not in any way 'spill over' into the 1, 4, 2, 8, 5, 7 symbol. The movement of this symbol proceeds on its own around the 1, 4, 2, 8, 5, 7 route from one type to the next. There is no point where we suddenly jump into the 3, 6, 9 triangle, or where the three points of the cosmic force of the triangle suddenly become essence types.

The 3, 6, 9 symbol represents *cosmic influence on all the types.* The numbers represent many different things. For example:

3: The force of the Being State, a conservative force which tends to preserve the original state of all created things (what some believe is 'real'); *stasis* – this also relates to the individual. (Venus types believe they can never change or be different.)

6: The Changing Corridor force of the planetary ray influence which constantly pulls at the entities in their Being State (their current state of being) to induce them to change (the 'Becoming' principle of change); *movement* – this also relates to the collective (it is on the side of the older types, who are non-personal, rather than the personal types on the right side of the Enneagram.

9: The Divine Universal Mind, which oversees all and influences the balance between change and stasis: *completion.*

The Divide

How are we best to understand The Divide that separates the 'younger' and 'older' types? Firstly, it is not so much a 'line', which is two-dimensional; rather it is a plane, but a *curved structure* that touches other cosmic force objects.

Secondly, 'younger' and 'older' is by no means the only defin-ition. Attempts to capture the properties and difference have also referred to them as 'lighter' and 'heavier'.

My teacher writes,

> There are certain traits in common that are shared by all the 'heavier' types, and certain other, sometimes (not always) opposite traits that are common to all the 'lighter' types.
> The closest I have come to having success referring to the two halves is to call the Lunar–Venus–Mercury types side the *Personal* side – since these signs are more concerned with everyday personal relationships, business relationships – things that are about *them*. The Saturn–Mars–Jupiter types side is the *Cosmic* side, since these people are more concerned with things that affect the planet, the world.
>
> There is also the definition of 'Personal' referring to Lunar–Venus–Mercury types who are concerned with what is in their personal world, themselves, their families, and so on. Whilst the 'Non-Personal' Saturn–Mars–Jupiter types are more concerned with abstract, vague principles that affect society, everyone, the 'out there' rather than the 'in here'.

We are also aware of the two hybrids that cross The Divide: Mercury–Saturn type and Jupiter–Lunar type. As is discussed elsewhere, the influence of one 'personal' and one 'non-personal' type-energy creates an individual with particular characteristics and life issues. For more on this consult what else is written in this book about these two hybrid types.

What Type Are You?

At this point you may feel ready to begin to determine your own essence type. All the information in the book up to this point is at your disposal.

When reading about the different types, one may have felt intuitively 'right' to describe you, or others you know. If this is so, do not rush too quickly into a definite conclusion – first review the information on such phenomena as operating out of type, type defaults, and so on. Working with the 12-type Ennea-gram is a serious business and *beginning from the wrong point* is clearly useless, even detrimental.

Consider:

- Would you say you were one of the *younger* or the *older* types? Do you tend to turn inward to the personal (Lunar, Venus, Mercury types) or are you not bothered with your inner world and are focused on the external (Saturn, Mars, Jupiter types)?

- This point is very important to understand. We tend to ignore our own type characteristics because they are so familiar to us (familiarity can breed contempt, even of ourselves). We admire particular characteristics of other types, not appreciating that if we were that type we would have *all* of its characteristics, positive and problematic. Clearly it is preferable for us to work to become a good representative of our actual type, and then to work consciously towards acquiring the positive characteristics of the next and other types.

    Intuitively going towards the next type means we may believe we *are* that type. Or we may believe that another type is more desirable than our own. My teacher recalls a class where the students each came in front of the group and stated their type. One person began 'Well . . . I'm a Saturn type' and was deluged by a cry of 'No! You're a Mercury type!' This also relates to type blindness – the individual cannot recognize their own type – *although outsiders can.*

- You may be a *hybrid*. This is distinctly different from moving towards the next type. There is a great difference between a Mars type, a Mars type who is well developed towards the Jupiter type, and a Mars–Jupiter type. The definitions make this clear. If you are wondering if you might be a hybrid, break down the different type-energies into their primary essence and it will be easier to determine whether or not you are dual-influenced:

Lunar	childlike
Venus	lover
Mercury	mover
Saturn	thinker
Mars	controller
Jupiter	universal carer.

These definitions are clearly not comprehensive but they may help you to think through your habitual ways of operating, and relating to the world.

- Consider the three sets of complementary types:

Lunar–Saturn	thinking
Venus–Jupiter	emotion
Mercury–Mars	movement.

  Which best covers your operating style?

- Might you be a split type? There are fewer split types than people who want to think of themselves as split types would imagine. My teacher relates the story of a young man who called himself a split Venus and Saturn type. He stated this in class but my teacher pointed out that his 'Saturn-type' insights were weak; in fact he was a Venus type who wanted to be thought of as intellectual. His self-belief was depriving him of access to the deep *emotional intelligence* that would be available to him as a good representative of Venus type. The moral here is that working to understand the value of one's own essence type is much more productive and useful than wanting to be admired for being something else.

  A true split type would manifest the characteristics of two non-consecutive types *equally*. Sometimes this occurs as an effort of will. For example, a woman who was a Venus type, through exposure to the 12-type Enneagram, consciously moved herself to Jupiter type (here we remember that both these types are similarly motivated by *love*).

- Be honest when you are *operating out of type*. As was noted in the first chapter, there can be dreadful consequences to not understanding your essence type and functioning in another energy for sustained periods. Here as well, it is not about finding the next, or any other type *more appealing*. We do not have control over many aspects of our lives and life generally. Deciding deliberately *to operate out of type* (for example, a Lunar type who wants to take a Mars-type job) will *not* make our lives happier. Our bodies are nourished by our being in our essence type so the longer we operate out of type, the more we deprive ourselves of essence-nourishing energy. In some cases this results in an unpleasant, ongoing rage (anger from the strain of the less-compatible energy being manifested) or depression (unhappiness causes the essence type to shut down).

Famous Faces

There are well-known people who accurately characterize the different types. Actors are often cast in roles that match their essence types. Consult the Internet for examples of them in films and off-screen, particularly accepting awards. Here are some famous faces matched with their types:

Lunar type	Audrey Hepburn
Lunar–Venus type	Marilyn Monroe
Venus type	Elizabeth Taylor
Venus–Mercury type	John F Kennedy
Mercury type	Danny Kaye
Mercury–Saturn type	Groucho Marx
Saturn type	Sigmund Freud
Saturn–Mars type	Churchill/Hitler/Stalin
Mars type	Clark Gable
Mars–Jupiter type	Nelson Mandela
Jupiter type	Ingrid Bergman
Jupiter–Lunar type	Grace Kelly

Once you have studied different examples of the types, which one reminds you of yourself? This exercise is not about identifying with celebrities or being flattered that you have the characteristics of someone famous. It is a means to study different types using icons who embody the different essence-type characteristics.

The Types Identification Test

I am a Person Who:

- **a:** Needs to dream and play my way through life
- **b:** Believes love and feelings are the most important things
- **c:** Talks fast and jumps around topics
- **d:** Enjoys questioning and discovering things
- **e:** Seeks a leadership role and influence over others
- **f:** Is concerned for the welfare of others

I am a Person Who Likes:

a: Bright colours and sparkling objects

b: Sensuous clothes, perfume or cologne and always looking my best

c: To know the latest trends/restaurants/gadgets

d: Discovering worthwhile books and places to visit

e: Challenge and goals and the loyalty of others

f: Bringing peace and harmony to my friends and surroundings

I am a Person Who Dislikes:

a: Being ordered around and having to keep to a routine

b: Vulgar behaviour and rude people

c: Never having enough time to do everything I want to

d: People who do not take things seriously

e: Being opposed or not getting my way

f: Cruelty, war and the terrible things going on in life

Because we have *all* the energies in us, to a certain extent all of these statements will be true for you. Look to identify the *essence*. Rather than spreading out over several letters, work to create a group of the *same* letter. Once you have a particular letter, it is most likely you are:

a: Lunar type

b: Venus type

c: Mercury type

d: Saturn type

e: Mars type

f: Jupiter type

However if you really are having difficulty, you may be a hybrid type:

I am a Person Who:

a: Loves being sexy and flirting

b: Feels deeply and likes to keep up with lots of friends

c: Has a high output and is interested in a million things

d: Has a deep sense of importance and a desire to become prominent

e: Will self-sacrifice for the greater goal

f: Is highly competent but sometimes wishes someone would look after me

I am a Person Who Likes:

a: Living on the edge of safety and security
b: Order out of chaos and feeling safe and protected
c: Complicated personal scenarios where I can explore
d: The opportunity to line up others to my way of thinking
e: Taking on inequality and contributing to social and political objectives
f: Taking care of friends and having time for myself

I am a Person Who Dislikes:

a: Inappropriate people and situations where I am sexually exploited
b: Being put down and made to feel unattractive/stupid/mean
c: Others not understanding that I am exploring life from my own point of view
d: Being thwarted, plotted against or out-manoeuvred
e: Injustice, prejudice, inequality and general passivity towards these evils
f: People not understanding my complex inner motivations and my selfless warmth for others

> **a:** Lunar–Venus type
> **b:** Venus–Mercury type
> **c:** Mercury–Saturn type
> **d:** Saturn–Mars type
> **e:** Mars–Jupiter type
> **f:** Jupiter–Lunar type

Again the process is the same: to bring together one of the letters attached to these statements that represents what is *most essential* within you.

Once you have made a *tentative* decision on which essence type you are, read this book *from that essence type's point of view.* You will soon realize if you have made a mistake because you will start to feel uneasy or sense that the information being given doesn't really correspond with what you are most deeply.

If you have made a false determination (remember to consult the list of factors that might be contributing to this) consider that any time spent with the 12-type Enneagram is never wasted. Even if you are not that type, you have still spent some time getting to recognize the type's characteristics. This will prove valuable when you begin to observe other people and start to make tentative observations about their type.

In the next section of the book we turn our attention to others in your life. Which type are, or were, your parents? Which types of friends are in your circle, and which not? And given your type, which types are most suited for a love relationship, and which are best avoided?

PART TWO

Applying the Enneagram to Others

Chapter 6

Family Structure and Enneagram Types

The life we experience growing up is, obviously, highly influenced by, and dependent on our parents. Did we have two parents, who loved each other? Was there only one parent, or were we raised in care, or adopted? Was there a divorce? Was there a lack of love? Were one or both distant, or angry, or controlling? We may believe we have already made sense of our circumstances, even made our peace – but now we will consider our upbringing in the light of the new information available through the 12-type Enneagram.

We are already aware of how different the experience of growing up can be for each individual child-now-adult. Many factors are involved, including the number of geographical moves and schools, number of siblings, or lack of them, whether or not the individual was gay growing up in a potentially hostile heterosexual family unit. Plus what is our racial profile and was that a positive, negative or neutral influence? To these traditional questions we now also need to consider that the experience of childhood will be different for one sibling from another *depending on their type*. So, for example, a Lunar-type child growing up in a Lunar-type family will be *differently equipped* for the family environment than would be a Mars-type child growing up in the same family. Each of the following descriptions includes notice of the child types, so we attain the fullest picture of the family type-dynamic.

Some Descriptions of Parental Essence Types

It stands to reason that a childhood lived with a Jupiter-type mother and a Saturn-type father will be markedly different from a childhood with a Venus-type mother and a Mars-type father. Or two Saturn-type parents, or a Lunar or Saturn or whatever type single parent. When we begin to examine what effect different parental types will have had on our childhood we gain new insight into our family-of-origin experience. Below are some real-life scenarios:

- **Lunar-type father, Lunar-type mother.** Both wanted the other to give them Venus-type love and support, which neither understood, leading to both becoming disappointed and angry. The influence of Lunar-type *self-obsession* created a family in which each person became responsible for their own emotional survival: there was insufficient 'benevolent parental containment'. Interestingly, of the four children, three are Lunar type as well; the other is Mars type. Mars has difficulty with Lunar-type energy, so for this child, living in a Lunar-type family with the resulting 'whimsical', 'isolated' family dynamic, brought about a particularly strong loathing for 'playing' and a desire for absolute control (not softened by Jupiter-type influence).

- **Mars-type father, Venus–Mercury mother.** The mother appreciated the father's ability to bring money into the family and she turned their home into an antique-and-art-filled showpiece. The mother was often absent from the home and did not truly appreciate the negative Mars-type influence of the father on the two children. The two children are Saturn type (girl) and Venus type (boy). Both suffered in different ways: the boy because he could not achieve what his father wanted, and was punished; the girl because she did not want to be 'girly' and subservient.

- **Jupiter-type mother, Saturn-type father.** Both are strongly religious, but able to argue logically (the mother accessed Saturn-type energy for disagreements with the father while the father went to Jupiter-type, not Mars-type energy, in conflict). Five children. All children grew up independent, active and resourceful. Much love towards, and received from, the children.

- **Mars-type father, Jupiter-type mother.** Two children, both Lunar type. The husband responded to the influence of the warm earth-mother wife and this was a happy family. The main issues were when the children grew to their own adulthood. Here we see that it is not *all* parental influence: the children's self-exploration led to some expensive mistakes and the parents sacrificed their own financial security to bail them out.
- **Saturn–Mars mother.** Divorced, highly prominent in the media. Children are loved but miss out on the one-on-one attention they crave; their mother has an important political/social agenda to fulfil and the children have experienced many examples of being placed second.
- **Lunar-type mother** (developed). Single parent. She is able to balance both a career in a high-paying creative field, and raising her two children, through disciplined, intuitive practice.
- **Venus-type husband, Mars-type wife.** Husband visibly younger (wife's second marriage). Wife's high-profile job requires the husband to raise their only child (boy: Venus type). Wife's choice of career (in charity) indicates a marked movement towards Jupiter type, and this is the energy she brings to her family. The husband is happy with raising their son; the wife is happy with a stable home and exciting career.
- **Mercury-type husband, Saturn-type wife.** Second marriage for both. Wife is aware of husband's scattiness and becomes angry when he breaks or loses something for the third time. However, she also appreciates that he was a late-life opportunity for her and is able to swallow her disappointment, given her understanding of the bigger picture. Both have adult children with lives of their own (types not known).
- **Lunar-type husband, Mars-type wife.** Two girls: one Venus type, one Saturn type. The husband attempted to be the dream mate he believed his wife wanted (which turned out to be another Mars type). Being Lunar type he ran out of energy and became angry and depressed. Wife responded by starting an affair, then leaving her husband for the other man, taking the children.

- **Saturn-type parents. Saturn-type daughter; Mercury–
  Saturn type son.** Both siblings benefited from focus on
  intellectual achievement and always knew they would
  succeed in intellectually demanding careers. Because
  the parents were not able to provide much emotional
  development modelling, children struggled with personal
  relationships. Son distanced himself geographically;
  daughter availed herself of therapy to learn how to fill the
  emotional gaps.

From reviewing these examples we can see how much of an unconscious, invisible influence parental essence types may have
had on our upbringing. What types do you think your parent or
parents are/were? In formulating an answer, please bear these
aspects in mind:

- Being in a relationship often moves the individual
  forward, but this may not be a permanent situation.
  Thus a Lunar type may appear for the first few years
  of the child's life to be a Venus or a Saturn type. As the
  demands of the child increase, the parent may revert to
  the spaciness and irresponsibility of Lunar type – and
  disappear or disappoint.
- The parent may be defeated by the limitations of their
  type. A Venus-type parent may rely on the children to
  bring themselves up since providing a Mercury-type
  environment, with clean clothes and organization, is
  beyond them. An undeveloped Saturn-type parent may
  feel vaguely concerned towards their child, but be aware
  that their intellectual abilities are not appropriate for the
  child's needs, so instead they withdraw, leaving the child
  to cope in an atmosphere of benign neglect.
- It is usually only with hindsight that the child can understand how the parent suffered. A Lunar-type parent may
  attempt to raise the child in a 'fairytale' reality; a Mercury-
  type parent may regard children as something entirely
  outside their understanding, and desperately thrust things
  at the children to cover up a sense of inadequacy.
- A Mars-type parent will demand obedience so a Venus-
  type child may have less of a problem, being acquiescent,
  than would a Mars-type child who may also adopt a

belligerent attitude. A Saturn–Mars type child will confuse a Venus- or Lunar-type parent since the parent won't understand from whence their child gets 'all their big ideas'.

A Cosmic Family Concept

This system is sympathetic to the idea that *we choose our parents*. Those of us whose parental influence has been difficult, harsh or virtually non-existent may resist this idea. Yet if we consider this life as part of a more complex set of life journeys the idea that we may have chosen difficult, dysfunctional, distant or cruel parental figures does make a kind of sense and, if we stay with the idea, this notion may bring the relationship with our parents into a new and more positive perspective.

In this life we are concerned with *this life*. The system does not encourage regression (the study of past lives). In this system the belief is that the curtain has come down on our past lives: it is this life on which we are wholly focused. However, we cannot help speculating that in a former life we, for example, may have been indifferent, absent or dysfunctional parents: perhaps this is why we have selected the parents we have in this life, in order to experience the relationship from the receiving end. But these thoughts can only ever be speculative: what is most important is the sense we can make of our parents and family in this life.

Also, this does not mean that if we have suffered, we should not do something to ease our distress and make sense of the past in this life. The notion of 'choosing our parents' does not cancel this out, but it does allow us to examine parental relationships in a different light.

Sibling Relationships in the Light of the Types

- A Lunar- or Venus-type daughter, in a family of boisterous Mars-type boys, will suffer. However, if the parents promote the daughter over the sons, the daughter may grow up with a warped sense of her own importance, while the boys will grow up feeling 'bad' inside.
- Twin Saturn types, a boy and a girl, are inseparable until the time comes for the boy to assert his independence from his twin (accessing Lunar-type energy). Having

taken the Venus-type energy from her twin for granted, the girl is left aching as her familiar ally develops beyond the family bond.

- A Lunar–Venus type boy is adored by his Mars-type sister until he wants a girlfriend. Then the sister wages war on every candidate.
- A Mars–Jupiter type son in a family of otherwise Lunar-type children cannot understand the 'secret world' the other siblings create; his wide external agenda is completely bewildering to them, and they politely ignore it, leaving him feeling unsupported and misunderstood.

Do or did you have siblings? What type would you say they are/were? Can you identify some of the type characteristics that were either helpful or difficult when you were growing up?

Observing Type Differences and Outcomes

It is fascinating to observe that two children of the same essence type, say Venus–Mercury type, may manifest the type characteristics in ways that would appear to make them polar opposites, *while in fact they are only manifesting the type characteristics differently*. For example, one Venus–Mercury type child falls in love with the drama of religion and becomes a monk: the other focuses on the luxurious rewards of working hard and plumps for a job in finance which enables him to indulge his love for expensive clothes.

Within the Lunar type there is a further complication. We take the example of a family where there are two Lunar-type children. The older one leaves school early, does a number of unrewarding jobs, and then returns to education, eventually going to university. So when the younger child also 'acts up', the parents encourage him also to leave school early, believing that the second child will follow the pattern of the first. But the first child is a Lunar-type B, who can benefit from the feedback life offers, and make the changes needed to be more successful in life, while the second is a Lunar-type A, who lacks the ability to gain knowledge through experience.

Another example is of a family where the two children are a Venus-type daughter and a Mars-type son. During their up-bringing, the Mars-type son bullies his sister, telling her that her opinions were not of any worth. So when she decides on a career in public relations, she is nervous of the intellectual content, but manages to acquire a qualification through speeding up to Mercury-type energy, and 'cramming' herself full of facts. Whereas her Mars-type brother, rather than knuckling down to his chosen career in teaching, becomes aggressive and antagonistic to the academic process involved (we remember that Mars types have academic pursuits in their previous energy) and drops out.

Where the type lies in the chronological order is also important. A Jupiter–Lunar type oldest daughter readily embraces the task of looking after her younger siblings. However, in another family, where the oldest child is a pure Lunar-type boy, the parents assume he will take on an early adult role, which he resents bitterly, and as an adult tells people that he 'never had a proper childhood'.

Where the Parent is 'Younger', the Child 'Older'

At first glance it might appear that in the parent–child dyad, the best relationship flows from a situation where the parent is one of the 'older' types (Saturn, Mars, Jupiter or one of the hybrid types) and the child is one of the 'younger' types, (Lunar, Venus, Mercury or, again, one of the hybrid types). However, obviously, the child does not always remain in the more vulnerable, learning state, and therefore it is not, in terms of the overall parent/child relationship, always an advantage. Indeed, some children report that their dominating parent turned from an asset to a liability as they strove to establish their own identity.

We should bear this in mind when considering the circumstance where the parent is 'younger' and the child is 'older'; although it may be confusing for the child growing up, it might in the long picture help them establish their true identity earlier. What sort of consequences may we expect to result from the parent being a younger type, the child an older type?

- **Lunar-type parents, Saturn-type daughter.** For the first few years the daughter enjoys the cosy, make-believe world the parents have created. When the daughter begins to visit her friends at their own homes she observes the differences in the family interactions. She steps away from the self-created world, instead launching on her lifelong investigation into the way life actually is. She learns to love her parents as basically eternally childlike, and to find intellectual guidance at school, where she excels academically. Her parents sweetly reassure her that they will love her no matter what a mess she makes of her life, while not appreciating that she is forging a worthwhile life for herself. Finally, as her parents age, she takes on the role of benevolent parent to them and they relax, relieved at being looked after by someone who knows them well.

- **Venus-type parents, Mars-type son.** The Venus-type parents raise their child to appreciate the joys of life to be found in beauty, stillness and one-to-one relationships. The son soon carves out his own little fiefdom, delighting in distressing his parents by his rough and abrasive manner. The parents have to learn to protect themselves and by the time he is a teenager he controls the power in the household. Yet because Mars types often value good family ties, he does not alienate them too much. His achievements on the sports field and his popularity with his peers and girlfriends are offered as trophies to his parents. They come to appreciate that he is very different from them, and he learns to regard them with tenderness and compassion (moving towards Jupiter-type energy).

- **Mercury-type father, Mars–Jupiter type daughter.** As often happens with the Mars–Jupiter type, it takes time for the daughter to discover the pursuits that give her life meaning and purpose. For a brief while she imitates her father's speedy and sometimes chaotic patterns but she learns early on they do not suit her. She observes how her father can become overwhelmed by too many demands, so she takes care not to share too much of her ambitions. As the daughter becomes prominent, the father learns to stand back and admire rather than interfere (Mercury types are busily involved in their own life and are content with keeping friends up to date with their achievements).

These three examples work out positively. There are other, less rewarding combinations:

- **Lunar–Venus type mother, Saturn-type son.** Being
  a deep-thinking, sensitive boy, he finds his mother's
  reckless emotional behaviour particularly distressing. As
  soon as he can, he seeks to be the solid counsellor she
  can rely on. She repays his devotion by making him the
  'reason' for all her disappointments.
- **Jupiter-type daughter, Venus-type parents.** The parents
  cannot understand their daughter's distress over homeless
  pets, floods in Asia and other everyday tragedies. They
  tell her she is only 'putting on an act' and that underneath
  she is 'just like them'. This causes the daughter even more
  distress as she becomes convinced she is worthless, and
  she works ever harder to feel acceptable.
- **Mercury—Saturn type son, Lunar-type parents.** The
  son has to defy his parental script ('anything for a quiet
  life') in order to find a focus for his energy. Since the
  parents often sabotaged their own opportunities through a
  combination of childish whimsy and reckless indulgence,
  the son has to learn to follow his own voice rather than
  listen to theirs.

Finally there is the example of a young boy whose birth mother gives him away. He is raised in care, which is often brutal, and grows up with a fierce determination never to compromise his independence. He is a Lunar type. Had he had the benefit of a loving family, he might have learned to move towards Venus-type energy and the one-to-one happiness of a committed relationship. Instead his many years of neglectful treatment make him chronically incapable of forming the intimate relationship he craves deeply.

Although we enter this world naked and alone our lives are never lived in isolation. Even if a parent is absent, or we are raised in care, we are surrounded by older people in the caretaker role, and that means we cannot escape the influence of other types – whether or not they understand what 'caretaking' requires. In the next chapter we will address the issue of the family we make for ourselves: our friendships.

Chapter 7

Friends and Friendships

Free of blood ties, we sew together a patchwork of relationships that, by the time of our mature years, comes to represent
various moments, stages and periods in our lives. It is always
fascinating, at a wedding, an anniversary or, sadly, a funeral,
to see the variety of people who have been gathered together to
make someone's journey through the years warmer and more
meaningful. We are already aware of the people who make up
our circle of friends: now we will examine these in the light of
the types, and how the influence of different types can enhance
or hamper our experience of life.

A. Childhood Friendships
Unacknowledged Sympathetic/Unsympathetic Factors

Sympathetic: A woman has known her best friend since
childhood. Twenty years ago the friend bought the house
next door, and the two women now continue to live,
with their husbands and children, in contented, lifelong
friendship.
Unsympathetic: A man's parents moved often throughout
his childhood, which meant ending one set of friendships
and looking for another in the new area, so he has come to
understand friendship as something that will always end.

In widening our understanding of the examples above
we factor in that the two women were able to maintain the
friendship because when they were growing up, neither of
the families moved. In adulthood, the two women were of a
demeanour that did not seek to travel and settle elsewhere, and
they both married men who were content to stay where they

were. Therefore, invisibly underpinning the friendship was a beneficial arrangement of type harmonies. Coming from stable backgrounds, the two women picked stable partners; thus the lifelong friendship was possible partly because of external factors. The man whose parents moved often *may* have been capable of a similar lifelong friendship, but the influence of his parental type made it impossible. Lunar types may move more often, and move on a whim or little real need; Mercury types will move for a new outlook, and Mars types to signal to others an improvement in their status. Jupiter types may move to be closer to worthwhile projects; perhaps it is only the Venus and Saturn types who tend to stay in one place.

Thus, in seeking to understand our own ability to form friendships in childhood, we must first consider what our family pattern gave or withheld, made possible or denied us. From there we can examine the friendships we *have* made, both those in childhood/adolescence/university – what can be considered the 'closed world', and those in adulthood, where the rules are different because we are less bound together by circumstances of geography or shared pursuit – the 'open world'.

Which Enneagram Types have Outlasted our Relationship Predictions?

There are two principal areas of focus here. First is ourselves: which type we are, because that has an enormous bearing on the friendships we will enjoy. Second is which types we are attracted to, and here the focus is on the other person or persons.

Ourselves by Type

Lunar type: Charming, childlike, may make friends easily, but unless we move to Venus-type energy, the bonds of friendship may not be maintained.

Lunar–Venus type: We look for friends who understand us, and help us: often these are people who accept our last-minute changes of schedule. We learn to shun those who pretend friendship while wanting to take sexual advantage.

Venus type: We focus, principally, on one 'best friend'. Growing up, our agenda is on gaining friends of attractive physical appearance, with money to spend on clothes and the other accoutrements that make someone popular.

Venus–Mercury type: We pursue lots of different friendships and prove to be a long-standing, loyal friend.

Mercury type: We pursue a number of interesting friendships. We value people who accept us as we are and do not criticize our sometime absence due to double-booking.

Mercury–Saturn type: Our friends are attracted by our energy and enthusiasm but we may keep them at a distance while we pursue our own agenda.

Saturn type: We like to explore and share with similar enquiring minds. We look for acolytes we can educate, or someone who shares our enthusiasm for the arcane.

Saturn–Mars type: We gather friends without much effort; they are attracted to our being 'cool', charismatic and the centre of attention.

Mars type: Our friendships involve hierarchy, with ourselves at the top or centre, and we will test our friends to ensure their loyalty. A balance of sporting friends from school and college, plus relationships we have forged through business makes up our friendship circle.

Mars–Jupiter type: At school and university we are politically and socially active and our friends are the by-product of our interests.

Jupiter type: We support a number of friends. We like people with complicated lives where we can help, and in this way we don't have to suffer having the spotlight on us.

Jupiter–Lunar type: We find it difficult to relate to people simplistically because we are complex: parent *and* child. We tend to parent most of our friends, it may be safer than revealing our own insecurities.

Our Friends by Type

Depending on what type we are, we will attract, or fail to attract, other types:

Lunar types: Make fun, attractive friends, but they may be difficult to pin to a time and we may have to organize (Mercury-type energy) our meetings.

Lunar–Venus types: Unless we have known them a very long time, they tend to be casual about arrangements and they will drop us for some passing sexual liaison.

Venus types: Excellent for maintaining friendships. However, we may be discreetly dropped if they decide we are not
on their material or physical appearance level.

Venus–Mercury types: Great fun and for such a busy type,
surprisingly emotionally present. We should not be jealous
of their other friendships since they value each friendship
equally.

Mercury types: Not everyone 'gets' this fast type's operating
style but this type is loyal to those who do. Remembering
this type's multi-interests, they may remain quiet about their
exploits until specifically asked.

Mercury–Saturn types: If we fit in with their current focus
they will be attentive and reliable. If they move on or if paths
diverge they find keeping contact difficult.

Saturn types: They may not be in contact for a while because
this anti-social type is working on some project. However,
they *give* a great deal when they do engage in friendship.

Saturn–Mars types: We don't try to compete; instead we
accept and enjoy being part of their retinue.

Mars types: Are benevolent and supportive while we
are getting on with our own lives. If we are successful, a
developed Mars type, moving towards Jupiter type, will be
particularly proud of us.

Mars–Jupiter types: We feel privileged to call them friend.
If we invite them to dinner they may ask to bring others with
whom they are working (and who will also be worthwhile).

Jupiter types: The warmest reception. We can rely on their
innate good-will. We must be careful not to take advantage
because they, being 'always benevolent', will do more than
their 'fair share'.

Jupiter–Lunar types: We can rely on this hybrid type too.
Sometimes we will not 'catch' their vulnerability, and may
suddenly be surprised when they throw a 'meltdown' of self-
doubt.

Taking these observations above as only a general guide, we now
have information to answer the question: *Which Enneagram
types have outlasted your friendship predictions?*

Remember it's partly your type, partly their type, partly circumstances and partly synchronicity or the lack of it. The Internet has reshaped and enlarged our ability to maintain friendships

and also created new friendship categories. The circumstances and demands of our technological age drive us towards more and surface relationships. Much of the time we function in 'pseudo-Mercury' type energy, which is unsubstantial and unsupportive.

Pursuing Adult Friendships

Once the circumstances of education and restrictions of geo-graphical movement have resulted in either the possibility or the impossibility of 'lifelong' friendships, adulthood offers another opportunity to create a circle of meaningful friendships. The qualities or limitations/unconscious compulsions in the 12 types, as already explored, will again influence adult friendships.

All the types, in adulthood, may make the necessary type limitation/compulsion adjustments necessary in order to forge more lasting friendships; this would be part of their becoming a *good representative* of their type, an *evolved* as opposed to an *unaware* individual. Lunar types may recognize that there is proper worth in coming out of their habitual self-obsession/absorption in order to maintain a warm connection with someone else (accessing Venus-type energy). Mars types may come to appreciate the value of not antagonizing friends, and instead move towards Jupiter-type benevolence in their friendships. It is not necessary to run through all the types again, since having defined the various attitudes towards friendships of both the individual and their friends, we can now move to friendships that are not actually what they seem.

Which 'Friendships' Are Not Working?

What confused-type people may we have had in our category of 'friends' who might not belong there?

> **Lunar type:** A Lunar type, kind as is characteristic, had
> to accept that a relative by marriage just did not like or
> appreciate them. Having made excuses over the years for the
> other's abrasive style (an unfortunate Mars-type energy), they
> needed to recognize the wisdom of the biblical quote 'I have
> gathered a serpent to my bosom' and break the connection.
> **Venus type:** A Venus-type woman recently finally broke off a
> 'friendship' that had been an emotional drain. Her friend was
> not interested in talking through her problems and solving

them, rather in spending evening after evening crying over a broken relationship going back years into the past. The Venus-type woman, even with the enormous capacity of her type for listening to other people's troubles, realized that there was *no value* in her listening because the friend was merely acting out some sort of inner compulsion to regard her life as miserable and helpless.

Mercury type: A Mercury-type man realized that a friendship was based only on his running around and organizing life for the other person.

Saturn type: A Saturn-type woman came to understand that it was not her conversation that was valued, but the guest room she offered a friend from the country: she decided to reserve her room, and her conversation, for those who appreciated them.

Mars type: A Mars-type man came to see he had been outplayed: the friend pretended to think he was wonderful, and took advantage of his material possessions, while at the same time mocking him behind his back.

Jupiter type: A Jupiter-type woman realized it was best to stop looking after a friend who was perfectly capable of doing it for herself.

These are all examples of how different types may fall into a friendship trap.

What Type Aspects are being Serviced in Friendship?

Because we all have all the types in us, and we have, historically, bounced unconsciously around the 12-type Enneagram, it is unlikely that we will be exactly the same friend to everyone we know, or that they will be the same with others as with us. *Different type aspects emerge in different friendships.* Of course, given our essence-type characteristics, there will be *some* limits and patterns to how we manifest our type-energies, but it is useful to think about whether we are benefiting from the type-aspects different individuals bring out in us.

Overall, it is often most helpful for us to associate with people who are of the next type, in order to learn for ourselves how they operate. Yet it is not necessary for friendship to be that prescriptive. Generally, our friends either *reinforce* our type characteristics, or *contrast* with them. This is not always a positive state of events. We may be servicing particular type-aspects in ourselves, and the other, *negatively*. Let us look at positive and negative examples.

Main-type Examples of Positive Type-Aspect Servicing

Lunar type: A Lunar type may be friends with a Venus type. While under the influence of Venus-type self-caring they will temporarily forget about their inner world and instead 'wake up' to focus on their physical appearance and matters of practical self-care.

Venus type: They may form a friendship with a Saturn type. The Venus type enjoys praising the Saturn type's deep insights and the Saturn type enjoys seeing life from a different perspective.

Mercury type: A Mercury type, struggling to make their way in the world, may become friends with a bookish Saturn type. The Mercury type benefits from being required to slow down, and the Saturn type is pleased to have the Mercury type's appreciation of their slower, deeper, take on life.

Saturn type: Saturn type will not always wish to relate to a friend in Saturn-type energy. They may deliberately seek out friends who are a relaxing opposite, spending a carefree evening with a rowdy beer-swilling pub mate, who could be a Mars type, or watching cartoons with a Lunar type.

Mars type: Even the most buttoned-up Mars type may have friends, particularly friends of long standing, with whom they can let down their hair. Here they are accessing and communicating along Lunar- and Venus-type energy lines.

Jupiter type: Jupiter type's generous and humorous nature often attracts Mars-energy types. Once the Jupiter type has passed the Mars type's 'audition for friendship', the Mars type appreciates their direct and sometimes abrasive manner being 'understood'.

More Negative or Harmful Different Type-Aspect Servicing

Where people antagonize or magnify the negative aspects of a type, the friendship can be considered 'negative' or even 'toxic'. This is often the case when types are related to in their *own* energy.

Lunar type: Two Lunar types in a friendship can exacerbate the spaciness and panic of the type, creating a friendship full of drama and imaginary paranoid terror.

Venus type: Two Venus types may be drawn into a whirlpool of competition based on appearance and material possessions (as in *The Real Housewives* reality TV franchise).

Mercury type: Relating to a Mercury type with Mercury-type energy increases the type's continual restless movement. Leads to a mirrored franticness with little calm.

Saturn type: Matching Saturn type's traits of solitude and secrecy can result in a friendship where there is virtually no access or joy.

Mars type: Two Mars types may compete. Meetings become a relentless jockeying for advantage, with both locked in an airless, desperate battle for dominance even though they may just be meeting for 'cocktails and a chat'.

Jupiter type: For a Jupiter type to be offered Jupiter-type energy may confuse them.

Additionally, it may be that a particular friendship brings out only a narrow range of energy-type influences:

Lunar type: You may be acceptable as a friend *only* when you are being the bouncy, charming childlike adult. *Or* it may be demanded of a Lunar type that they be always upbeat.

Venus type: You may be acceptable as a friend *only* when your life is going well and you are looking good. *Or* you may only contact a Venus-type friend when you know they are in funds and can join you in a financial splash.

Mercury type: You may be acceptable *only* when you are *doing* something for someone else. *Or* you may call your Mercury-type friend only when you want a favour.

Saturn type: You may be acceptable *only* when you can explain something. *Or* you call your Saturn-type friend only when you want them to help you out with the same sort of problem.

Mars type: You may be acceptable *only* when you can take charge of a situation. *Or* you may only contact your Mars-type friend when you want them to back you up in a dispute.

> **Jupiter type:** You may be acceptable *only* when someone needs a big hug. *Or* you may contact your Jupiter-type friend only when you need a shoulder to cry on.

Beware of having only one type of friend. For example, if you are a Venus type, and you find it easy to attract other Venus types, that situation may work well when you're talking shopping, but when you have a personal crisis your 'undeveloped' Venus-type friends may melt away: 'fair-weather friends'. Better also to develop friendships with Lunar types (can be very loyal), Mercury types (can help with organizing moving day), Jupiter types (always ready to comfort).

Now that you have been introduced to the 12 types, think about the desirability of picking friends *informed by their essence-type characteristics* such as a Jupiter type for support, a Mars type for the inspiration to take charge, a Lunar, Lunar–Venus or Venus–Mercury type for cheering up. However, this should never be one-sided. It is one thing to make friends while consciously considering the information available through the 12-type Enneagram; it would be a corruption of this information to calculate and manipulate friendships for your own ends.

Avoiding Learning from Types

As has already been noted, we gain enormously from observing the type ahead of us, and learning how to think, feel and behave as they do. Also, someone who is a distant type from us may be doing exactly what would help us. Yet, hitherto, without the benefit of the 12-type Enneagram, we may be doing all we can to avoid looking at, or thinking about this fact. Inside us there are *lazy mechanisms* with no interest in improving – all they can feel is the pain of having to make the effort. So, even if we know *what* we should be doing, the *effort, or fear of the pain of making the effort,* puts us off.

Yet this doesn't mean we aren't, in any case, suffering. We spend more energy avoiding what we should do than we would learning how to put it into practice. There are, in fact, two types of pain. The one is useless mechanical pain that goes round and round in a profitless dirge. The second type is the pain involved in applying some degree of conscious effort to the situation. This is the pain that heals. When we have learned to do whatever it is we need, *it goes away* – leaving us able to function in a better way.

So, rather than shy away, or avoid, those people who we may know are offering us something we need, we could think, 'This person brings up some resistance or conflict in me, yet I know they have something to teach me. I will try to make a friend out of them. I will experiment *with myself* to see what works with them.'

By this last point, we acknowledge that it may be something in us that's causing the problem. For example, a Lunar–Venus type may instinctively shy away from a Jupiter type because the Jupiter type offers them unconditional support, not pleasant sexual tension/gratification. The Lunar–Venus type, by recognizing that he/she has a limited circle of friends, begins to try to learn what it is the Jupiter type is offering by feeling it in themselves. Or a Mars–Jupiter type, constantly battling for an ideal, may realize that the giggly presence of an acquaintance (Lunar type) is what they need for light relief, and seeks out the Lunar type so they can learn to find/do it for themselves.

Negative Identification

It may be that the person *reflects* or *symbolizes* something about ourselves that we don't like. So we avoid them, just as we avoid acknowledging and dealing with that part of ourselves. As well, by consciously deciding to make a friend out of someone who has a problem area similar to our own, we have the opportunity of seeing the situation *more objectively*. We all are capable of seeing what other people are doing wrong; by having a friend with the same issues as ourselves, we can learn what the problem really is, and by knowing the characteristics of the 12 types, we can add the missing energy influence:

- Jeannie (Mercury type), appears to be proud of her ability to fire out three or four conversation topics at once. Privately, after a night out, Jeannie weeps and blames herself for her uncontrolled chatter, which she knows irritates her friends. She meets Kevin, also a Mercury type, who has a similar pattern, and Jeannie makes a point of listening to him. By seeing his triggers, by observing his inability to keep to a single point, Jeannie realizes how she can help herself (and she has slowed herself down, taking her more towards Saturn-type energy).

- Deal, a Mars type, knows he can fight the fight but he is tired of the relentless posturing and posing. He starts to listen to his best friend, Ryan, and sees how much energy Ryan wastes in useless point-scoring. Deal resolves to do something worthwhile with his energy (accessing Mars–Jupiter type energy).

Once we are working with the 12-type Enneagram we begin to appreciate that other people's irritations are in fact opportunities to work on ourselves.

Using the Enneagram to Understand Friendships

By being aware of the different type-energies, we can add whatever is missing to a friendship, or understand why it could not survive.

There are different kinds and degrees of friendships. Some are situational – the people we meet at the supermarket or the gym. Others are work-based, and when we leave the company, we never expect to see our co-workers again. Depending on our type, though, we may stay friends. Lunar types are less likely to, although individuals are very loyal to specific friendships; Venus, Venus–Mercury, Jupiter and Jupiter–Lunar types are more likely to maintain old work contacts and meet up socially. Some Mars types will stay in touch, though often principally for networking opportunities (which they would never think exploitive).

Another example of the usefulness of the 12-type Enneagram is in understanding that *all six energy types are necessary for a proper friendship.*

> **Lunar-type energy:** This is where the friendship begins.
> **Venus-type energy:** Provides the emotional connection that supports the friendship.
> **Mercury-type energy:** The organization needed to set up meetings and so on.
> **Saturn-type energy:** Deepens the relationship.
> **Mars-type energy:** The sense of 'owning' the friendship, of it being an important part of the total of our relationships.

Jupiter-type energy: The benevolent support and sense of reward we get both from the friend and from our contribution and commitment to the friendship.

If we look at the six different energies, all necessary, we understand why some friendships fizzle out or go wrong:

We meet someone at work and start hanging out together, talking about business. This is Lunar- and Mars-type energy – but the others are missing. There's no real emotional connection (lack of Venus-type energy); we meet only because it is convenient (lack of Mercury-type energy); we don't talk about anything heavy or serious (lack of depth: Saturn-type energy); we don't *value* the friendship, we see it as purely geographical (lack of Jupiter-type energy).

At the end of a love affair we determine to continue the relationship 'as friends'. It fizzles out abruptly. This is because there was plenty of Venus-type energy, but not enough accepting Jupiter-type energy – the *sincere* desire for the other person to be happy – to offset the sexual jealousy or thwarted desire still remaining from the affair.

We jog and one morning we meet another jogger. We resolve to jog together. After a few months they do not show up and we never see them again. That is because there was plenty of Mercury-type energy, plus some Lunar-type pleasure in making jokes together, and even some Mars-type energy in achieving our goals. But there was no Saturn-type energy to question what we were doing, or Venus-type energy for us to value the other person.

We aspire to being friends with someone with a higher profile than ourselves. Although we believe we have something of worth to offer them, it doesn't feel equal. We feel we can't protest because the bond between us is so paper-thin. From them there is no sense of Mars-type *owning* energy for the friendship, or Venus-type warmth, seeing how much we want to be friends. They may be in self-obsessed Lunar or Saturn–Mars type energy, and we may decide to regain our dignity by dumping them (the occasionally satisfying result of applying a little Mars-type energy).

If you decide to examine your own friendships, look for signs of where the energies of the six types are present, and if you realize the friendship is lacking, consciously seek to add those energy components.

Transforming Our Friendships

We live in a time when electronic communication has fundamentally changed the way we operate and experience things. Yet the concept of 'Internet friends' is only a 21st-century interpretation of the old 'pen pals'. In the last few years, particularly in urban centres, the concept of *a friendship circle* has become popular. A group, more often young women than men, gets together and deliberately choose to form a bond with their peers. Traditionally, in rural communities and small towns, we made friends with whoever was around and available, a fact that led to a greater tolerance of the foibles of others, and a greater acceptance of difference, both of which are Venus-and-Jupiter-type processes. The friendship circle is an attempt in an urban setting to recreate the intimacy and acceptance of smaller communities.

Whether or not we deliberately set out to create a friendship circle, from the 12-type Enneagram point of view it is valuable to bring people around us who enhance and support us, *including an understanding of which types will be good in our lives*. It is easy for us to see the point in having friends who are the same type as us. It may be harder to understand why we need to seek out people who are other types. Now we understand that we can use those around us in a positive way to grow ourselves; we can let go of friendships that are not good for us, and from our growing understanding of what we can bring to friendships, we can create a network for ourselves that is strong, emotionally supportive and reliable for the good times and the difficult phases in our lives.

PART THREE

Sex, Love and the Types

Chapter 8

Sex and the Types

Let's Talk About Sex

Now that I have your attention . . . and that is precisely the point of sex. Sex energy. All things sexual: *sex wakes us up*. That is why it is so useful in advertising: sex gets our attention. Put a pretty woman, or handsome man, in your ad and the public will be drawn to your product. Yet although sex wakes us up, it also keeps us in sleep; it binds us to a cycle of incremental sexual tension and orgasmic release, and after years of being in the spell of sex energy we may realize that the whole shebang is basically a distraction from serious or more meaningful pursuits. Yet deciding to do without, or not being able to get it when we want it, is often not a happy answer either. Sex is powerful, seductive, mysterious and – depending on the moment, the circumstances and the opportunity – we may go with it, push against it, deny it or lose ourselves in it.

We can understand it as that we manifest different varieties of energy: life energy, meditation energy, death energy and sex energy. In a book about energies it will not be surprising for us to learn that sex *is* an energy. Sex energy, the *forbidden fruit*, has the characteristics and constitution of a wild horse: uncontrolled, reckless and wayward – which is why religion and those who have their own problems may preach against it. This state of affairs is unfortunate: the cosmology discussed in this book is sympathetic to the idea that *sex energy is important and should not be wasted*. Nowadays research and exploration is being made into *kundalini* and *tantric* energy, both of which are associated with sex energy, although often these experiments are less scientific, more sensual. What is sex energy? Do we all have it? Do some of us have more of it than others? What is its purpose?

What is Sex Energy?

As previously stated, sex energy both wakes us up in a particular way, and keeps us asleep. It can best be understood as a *natural and inescapable by-product of life energy.* The joy we feel at having the sun on our skin, the excitement of completing something creative and achieving recognition, the touch of the right person: all these sensations celebrate life energy and also bring about the creation of some sex energy. This is why people who are creative tend to have more sex energy than others, and creative people will often struggle with this, if not concerning the sex act itself, then in finding a release for this potentially bothersome energy. This can become some form of addiction or fetish. Judges who wear women's underwear under their robes are attempting an unusual solution to a serious problem: how to keep themselves 'grounded' when every day they rule on peoples' lives.

The broker who cannot go home until he has paid for a lap dance and the female politician who masturbates between House of Commons' debates understand that sex energy can be used to let go of our other tensions. A well-known and prolific writer once bravely shared that when she is in the depths and heights of creativity she masturbates up to five times a day. We can interpret that writer's candour as *normalizing* the use of sex as a controlling device. It can also become addictive in itself. For example, a writer who becomes alcoholic may come to believe that the alcohol is necessary for creation. A singer develops a drug addiction to burn up the vast quantity of sex energy created by performing in front of an audience of many thousands. In these two examples, the joy of creativity may be outweighed by the price. But sex energy is also present in the office, on the Tube, at the dinner party. We know this, and yet normally we do not think about it to any great extent. We save it for the office Christmas party. We read about 'three-in-a-bed' or 'sex romps' and we do not appreciate this is a serious phenomenon that sometimes takes over peoples' lives. Whether or not we are plagued by sex energy, we can all benefit by understanding it better.

The spiritual teacher G I Gurdjieff suggested that we can divide our operating systems into different centres and nominated five as constituting our normal behaviour: intellectual, emotional, moving (for all our physical movements) and instinctive (for all the processes that should remain outside our consciousness, such as breathing). The fifth centre is the sex centre, and in keeping with its notorious reputation, it is more difficult to find information on this shadowy part of our psyche. For some people, the existence of a centre entirely devoted to sex sounds wonderful. Since research produces such findings as, for example, that whatever else they are doing, men think about sex every ten minutes, the notion that we do actually have an energy *devoted* to this pursuit may seem like hitting the permission jackpot. What is most interesting about this piece of information is that the process actually going on is that our psyche invites us to think about sex *as a means to help us* – with tension, boredom, when we have something to prepare for or when we need a distraction from ourselves.

There is also a higher purpose to our having sex energy; it can be used for *transformation*, rather than the varied, enjoyable, sometimes indulgent and often worthless and mechanical ways in which we use it. This is why sex keeps us asleep: thinking about sex and constructing our lives around sexual pursuits and rewards limits our horizon. This may be helpful in keeping the majority docile, but it means a great deal of energy is being wasted. By conquering or controlling the common manifestations of sex energy we *wake up* in a meaningful way; the sex energy can be transformed to heighten our consciousness. The energy not being used up in sex can be used to break through our usual barriers and into what Gurdjieff called the higher intellectual and higher emotional centres. This is the original, now mainly forgotten, purpose of sexual abstinence.

Where this leads to true spiritual enlightenment the reasoning is sound, but where it leads to 'hell and damnation' preachers being caught in adultery, consorting with prostitutes or sent to rehab for alcohol or other substance abuse, then the original intention can be seen as having been corrupted. Sex, as most of us already know, is powerful stuff, it is messy and embarrassing, and this is really how it should be. Who fantasises about sex with Mary Poppins? It is associated with words like 'dirty', 'sleazy', 'sordid' and 'vice' when what is really going on has the potential to be much more extraordinary than we give it credit for. It is used as an instrument of shame and to shame. 'Queer', 'poof', 'slut', 'whore': it is interesting that the only gender group not included is the white heterosexual male, who may instead rejoice in the sobriquets 'stud' and 'player'. Sex is used to control societies and bring down otherwise useful and powerful people; it is a handy Achilles heel when the person is otherwise impregnable.

A discussion on how the white male patriarchy has used sex to control and shame is outside the remit of this book. Additionally this chapter will not attempt to deal with the transformational aspect of sex energy other than to observe that such is a principal purpose of sex energy and the sex centre. Take the idea of the potential power of sex as an *impression*. In terms of the 12-type Enneagram we will limit ourselves to discussing the *ordinary* or *non-transformational* ways in which each of the essence types differently and typically regards the issue of sex.

Lunar Type

Sex is Magic. Lunar types are *inordinately* interested in sex. Not because they like the physical act so much, but because it makes them *feel alive,* and *wanted* by someone in the outside world (remembering the intense isolation in which Lunar types go through daily life). This type will spontaneously fantasise in a sexual way about people they have seen on the way to work, work colleagues, or people on television, and others.

However, this does not mean they are nature's 'sex maniacs'. Being childlike and innocent in their essence, the Lunar type may also feel very guilty about sex and sexual thoughts and believe themselves to be 'really quite sexually deformed' *without actually having sex*. Often it takes being in a relationship to move this type towards the sexual understanding available in Venus type, so they may have sex, get married, have children and *only then* realize the point of physical communion.

Lunar–Venus Type

Sex is Ambivalence. It was said of Lunar–Venus type Marilyn Monroe that she, who was perceived as the ultimate sex symbol, was actually 'sexually innocent'. The earthiness of Venus type, coupled with the free-wheeling independence of Lunar type creates a person irresistible to others but problematic to themselves. They are never sure exactly how much in control they are of sex, and although they use it liberally, they may not achieve personal happiness. They often start having sex earlier than the other types, so it is both something they are familiar with, and also something they believe they've 'done' in all its variations. Others find them frustrating because the Lunar–Venus type is both sexually magnetic and world (sex)-weary.

Venus Type

Sex is Paramount. Venus types 'live for love' and habitually they express that love through sex. Whereas for a Jupiter, Lunar or Saturn type the actual sex act is something complex, and they have ambivalent thoughts about it, for Venus type it is *central*, and unsatisfactory sex will probably be a deal-breaker.

Venus types express themselves through feelings and they may not realize that other types do not accord sex and emotion the same value. The woman who cries to her married lover on his departure, 'I don't understand – we made love in a rowing boat, you read me poetry!' is confusing a memorable moment with a permanent commitment; he is rejecting her because his ties to his family outweigh the importance of the sexual connection, which is a choice she does not understand.

Exposure to the 12-type Enneagram helps us to appreciate the kind of energy we need in intimate situations. Venus type operates at 72 beats a minute. Focusing on the physical presence of the other and ourselves will bring us into the Venus-type energy influence.

Venus–Mercury Type

Sex is Amusement. Unlike the first hybrid type, Lunar–Venus, this type has sex much more under control. Sex has its place, along with the other social functions this busy type enjoys. The influence of Mercury's speed may cause things to backfire sexually because this type may not be able, or willing, to slow down to the Venus-type pace.

Mercury Type

Sex is Flurried. With Venus type behind them, Mercury type tends to back off from sexual intimacy – too many distracting things going on – and they whiz through affection, hoping they are saying and doing the right thing, but giving sex the type's habitual superficial treatment. They are great finders of problems in relationships. They relate stories of petty misdemeanours that conclude with 'so of course we had to break up' and expect to be understood by other types. Other types (particularly Venus types) in fact cannot understand why *anyone* would throw away a whole relationship just for one thing that wasn't acceptable. By ignoring the value of sexual intimacy this type may find themselves relegated to the position of 'friend' rather than lover.

Mercury–Saturn Type

Sex is Sophistication. The influence of Saturn type creates a fast-moving person whose sexual interests may be secretive and experimental. Because they have learned to keep their cards close to their chests, the loved one may believe that they are un-complicated and not particularly bothered about sex. But under-neath, they believe getting sex right is very important, and at the proper time they may astound or horrify their partner, and social circle, by the unpredictable sexual moves and choices they make.

Saturn Type

Sex is Distraction. For this deep-thinking, questioning type, having to drop their intellectual pursuits and explorations in order to get physical begins as an irritation. Then as the type 'gets going', they enter into sex with the same depth and attention they give to other pursuits. Sex talk will be references to historical, contemporary and fictitious people and their sexual positions may have been learned from a book.

A Saturn type who has been exposed to the 12-type Ennea-gram will seek out sex for what they need: a Lunar-type experience for exploring lightness, a Venus-type for sensuous-ness and intimacy, a Mars-type for earthiness and a Jupiter-type when they want to be held and accepted.

Saturn–Mars Type

Sex is Empire-building. The seriousness of Saturn type coupled with the desire to be followed creates a type that uses sex for strategic goals. They will pursue a trophy wife or husband and prefer to do without rather than accept a mate who doesn't fit their high expectations. They may regard their friends' husbands/ wives as a series of potential conquests. Conversely, they may seek the seclusion of a warm and supportive family circle precisely because they do not want to compromise themselves sexually.

Mars Type

Sex is Possession. Building on the athleticism and sense of adventure embodied in the Mars-type energy, this type prides itself on sexual performance. Sex will definitely not be 'vanilla' but it may be curiously devoid of actual passion since demonstrating sex tricks and unusual, erotic diversities is the more important agenda. 'I love you' may be included but this type means something very different by it than does the Venus type: for the Mars type 'I love you' in a sexual context is a statement of ownership, not vulnerability.

Mars–Jupiter Type

Sex is Irrelevant. The loftier aims of this type tend to relegate sex to the sidelines. Sex, when it occurs, needs to be meaningful and is most often focused on creating a child. When a Mars– Jupiter type embraces sex for recreation or intimacy, they may reveal a surprisingly vulnerable, warm and sensitive aspect of themselves, which the lucky recipient will treasure.

Jupiter Type

Sex is Kindliness. Often this type will have sex to oblige the other party, rather than because they themselves are 'turned on'. Being located far from Venus type, they may need to have the purpose of sex *in itself* explained to them. Their sex and love partners often surprise because they are people who *need* them rather than their equals. Sex itself can be, if not disappointing, then at least *different* for the other party. Often it's a cuddly roll in the hay, with childlike 'play' rather than steamy abandonment.

Jupiter–Lunar Type

Sex is Genteel. Sexual attraction is not their chief attribute, since they are somewhere between a parent and a child. Being possessed of both, they regard sex as a warm, comfortable pastime and don't give it much emphasis. When experiencing the deep loneliness of Lunar type they may develop a craving for affection; by understanding how to access Venus-type energy they will overcome the parent/childlike adult block to lover status.

Casual Sex: One-Night Stands and Instant Gratification

Within each type group, individuals will function better, or worse, with this delicate issue.

> **Lunar types** don't tend to do well with anonymous/casual encounters because they habitually use sex to get what they really want: love, continuity of affection, security. However, once they have this, they will be perfectly able to have anonymous sex, secure in their primary relationship.
>
> **Lunar–Venus types** will *think* they want anonymous sex, but since they often don't choose well, this may become messy and disappointing.
>
> **Venus types** may flirt outrageously and keep this up for weeks or months. Because Venus types need to have everything tasteful and impeccable, the type is really not that keen on casual sex because it is not up to their standard of expectations. Gay male Venus types can have surprisingly few sexual encounters.
>
> **Venus–Mercury types** enjoy the encounter and make mental notes to tell their friends about the funny aspects. They may also not like the 'seamier' side so they blank this out by rushing off to the next appointment.
>
> **Mercury types** may enjoy the idea but the actual individual encounters blur into a whole. Often they tend to be not much interested, unless they can also impress the other party with their fascinating personalities/lives.
>
> **Mercury–Saturn types** like complicated scenarios which may work against one-nighters.
>
> **Saturn types** may have casual sex only when they've thought of every other solution to ennui.

Saturn–Mars types do not like the anonymity and view it only as a biological necessity.

Mars types may enjoy anonymous encounters or instant gratification and will stamp their control on it.

Mars–Jupiter types tend to eschew the issue because sex is not a simple matter for them.

Jupiter types will go along with casual sex if they need to, but they will look out, during the encounter, to make a *human* connection. They are disappointed if the other person is not interested in this dimension.

Jupiter–Lunar types may find the circumstances exciting, but afterwards they may be left with a sense of letting themselves down, or mostly be relieved that the encounter is over.

Again, certain individuals may not be wholly representative of 'type' and indeed individuals may operate outside of their type. For example, a Saturn type may default into Lunar type and, for all their intellectual sophistication, be irritating and unfocused in the sex act. This is because, although this is the 'questioning' type, they have not wanted to explore sex intellectually. By understanding sex from the point of view of the 12 types, we have the possibility of becoming better at sex, as well as appreciating our partners' confusions or difficulties (and helping them to overcome these by moving to a more useful type-energy).

The Sexual Carousel – or Roulette Wheel

The 12 descriptions above are only a brief sketch. The reality is infinitely more interesting and complicated. Sex really is a mystery, although we can quantify and qualify more than we realize – with information from the 12-type Enneagram. Here are some concluding thoughts.

A female acquaintance once complained that 'the problem with the good-looking ones is all they do *is lie there* and you have to do all the work'. Interpreted in the 12-type Enneagram, this would mean that the 'good-looking ones' are Venus types, who tend to be the still centre around which others revolve.

A person may be in the Venus type but in sex revert to Lunar type. This may because of historical trauma, religious guilt or a physical reason. Once this is understood it can be beneficial for the relationship, because a Venus type who lacks sexual confidence will be more likely to be faithful, less prone to elaborate sexual games and complex emotional scenarios.

A Lunar type, going forward to Venus type, may be better in bed than their physical frailty suggests. Conversely a body-builder (possibly Mars type) may be rock-like horizontally; in sexual matters, don't judge a book by its cover.

Mercury types need to have a giant hug, and be consciously slowed down, if they are going to enjoy sex. Inside the Mercury type's mind they are already racing ahead to other commitments and priorities – once we understand this propensity, we can help them to enjoy the *present* moment.

Saturn types may not focus on their physical requirements. The other party may be confused as to whether sex is actually going to happen. It may not be integrated, rather a function coming from another place.

Since the existence of the sex centre is true in all of us, whether or not we are sexually active, 'sex' remains an important factor. Unforeseen results may occur if we consciously try to block or kill off our sexual energy/drive, because other aspects of life, like a sense of well-being and sense of humour, are connected to sex. Thus someone who is consciously depriving themselves sexually, or who believes life has given them a raw sex deal, may become emotionally and sexually inflexible and bitter.

Younger types especially are prone to claiming (proudly apparently) that they are 'cynical' or 'bitter' – they need to be gently challenged. The truth is that these two unattractive adjectives are the result of their original hope and trust being thwarted, unwelcome or poisoned. Once these individuals understand that cynicism and bitterness are not the effective defences they fondly imagine, their original hope may re-emerge.

The lack of sex may turn people to overeating or to one of the underweight eating disorders. 'Comfort eating' is a misleadingly cosy description for what may have become the most important focal point in someone's life. Conversely, an individual may eat in order *not* to have to deal with sex – where sex feels overwhelming or frightening. This behaviour may be more common to Lunar types (rejection/confusion of adult role and responsibility) than other types.

A situation where sex is grounded on warmth, respect and a mutual need for physical contact and comfort is the best formula. Resist any negative Venus-type rebukes or criticism *inside and outside the bedroom* because nothing spells impotence or rejection like personal, physical put-downs.

Sexual abstinence can be highly rewarding for a limited time period. The emphasis needs to be on 'limited'. The writer Christopher Isherwood in *My Guru and His Disciple* relates how, after a period of six months' deliberate sexual abstinence, he was unable to function in his daily life due to distracting, spontaneous, sexual fantasies from his unused sex energy.

As we age the sex centre becomes increasingly less demanding. This may be a relief to some. It is not advised that we artificially force this downward turn any more than is required by our body. For some types in particular, maintaining an interest in sex is desirable for feeling good about ourselves, although we may choose imagination or sexually stimulating literature rather than seeking sexual contact.

It should be understood, finally, that we have been given sexual energy for a purpose (and not just the ability to produce children) so it needs to be appreciated and respected. Use the wisdom of Saturn type to make sense of sex, with some intuitive thoughts from Lunar type, and the emotional and physical intelligence of Venus type for beneficial results. The concept of 'worth' engages the Saturn-type energy and since it is so far from Venus type it allows for a mental distraction or change of emphasis which detaches you from the less attractive sex-aspects of the Venus-type energy.

Bothered by Sex Energy?

This mantra can help: 'I do not want sex to be the *meaning* of my day/evening/social life/friendships/relationships.' If we are feeling sexually aroused or frustrated and we can remember to think this, it will put the uncontrollable, wild energy back into perspective and we will be able to make more rational decisions on how to use our time.

Chapter 9

Love and the Types

The Relationship between Sex and Love

Historically, for the species to thrive, the female and the male needed to feel good as a consequence of sex. During the sex act, endorphins are released that have the biological function of bringing the two people closer together. This is nature's design, leading to the forming of more permanent bonds. However, as usually happens, humans historically complicated nature's plan by using sons and daughters of important families to bring about tribe and country alliances. For some, marriage was a political act. The church added its own demand that sex was sanctified only in marriage. Societal pressures and prohibitions also became factors in blurring the relationship between sex and love.

However, human beings are distinguished from most other forms of life in that we can fall in love and not only with a member of the opposite sex. For our organism, the mechanics and mysteries of love transcend the concept that love is a by-product of sex and that sex is only concerned with the act of procreation and species promulgation and protection. Nowadays lesbians and gay men, in the civilized countries of the world, are attaining proper equality with the right to bring up children and be married. As is probably already obvious, the 12-type Enneagram makes no distinction between heterosexual and homosexual love. The circumstances of an individual's sexuality do not affect their ability to fall in love and it will have no bearing on which type combination will be better and which less favourable. For each of us the pursuit of love and the maintenance of love is an individual quest and there are no guarantees. Yet by understanding one's essence type, and recognizing someone else's essence type, we are greatly helped in overcoming the many obstacles which appear to lie between us and a lasting, satisfying and worthwhile loving relationship.

Because each of the 12 types has unique characteristics and modes of thinking, feeling and behaving, each of the 12 has its own, unique way of looking at love. And of course since we have each of the type-energies within us, *in a relationship we may initiate or respond to the other person from any one of these 12*. This explains why some relationships start well and then go awry: either the type combination is incompatible, or the type operating misfires. Again, this is why the predictive ability of the 12-type Enneagram is so valuable: not only can we determine which types are more likely to lead to a successful match, we can also anticipate and integrate the expected movement from the other's essence type in relation to the type behaviour they access as a result of the relationship. Here we must bear in mind that we will also be affected by the relationship, and we must be aware also of the type towards which the relationship will take us, and the defaults which will be both our internal response and the external response to the other.

The Seven-Year Relationship Cycle

Part of my therapeutic work in love and relationships has led to my interest in the concept of a *seven-year relationship cycle*. The Marilyn Monroe vehicle *The Seven Year Itch* was a catchy but shallow interpretation of what is a much deeper and more important phenomenon: that there appears to be a definite rhythm and cycle to relationships, with predictable stress points. It is not a case of sudden change or a rush of boredom, but that throughout the years there are natural breaks when a relationship may go deeper and become more rooted, or become stale and static or end. I have explored this concept with certain of my psychotherapy clients and other interested parties and my informal research indicates that the stress points appear to be:

> 3 months
> 6 months
> 1 year

2 years
5 years
7 years – end and a new beginning

The *form* of interruption or break may change as the cycle progresses. For some relationships, external factors lead to an ending, for others the factors are internal. The cycle completes every seven years, at which point a new cycle begins or the relationship ends (relationships may also come to an organically natural end at 14 or 21 years or so on; again the cycle is complete). Each of the stages has its own characteristics, typically the level of intimacy which each partner and the unit is capable of and comfortable in maintaining. As suggested by the list of stress points within the seven-year cycle, it seems there are energies working either to promote, or to challenge, the relationship. A situation that can be contained when the relationship is in a positive phase may overwhelm the relationship if it takes place during a negative phase or at a stress point.

All types experience these stages; these are the periods when either the relationship grows deeper and more meaningful, or it fizzles out – sometimes with much anger from one or both parties if they initially had a positive reaction to the stress point. If we understand that we may just be in a time-stage of the relationship where we need more energy, more *reason* to stay in the relationship, then the stress point may be worked through. As well as predictable stress points, there is another factor that may play its part in the development or destruction of a relationship: *one or both of the partners may be operating out of their essence type.*

Consequences of Operating out of Essence Type

As has been noted previously, since up till this point most people have not had the wisdom of the 12-type Enneagram to guide them in being good representatives of their essence types, it is only to be expected that people are behaving out of their type. Firstly, someone may be operating in a different type, not their essence type, when the couple meet. For example, a Mars type may be operating in Jupiter type. The new interest may be attracted to the same qualities that the Mars type finds appealing about Jupiter type. When the two begin a relationship the Mars type will revert to their essence type and rather than the eternally benevolent Jupiter-type energy, the Mars type may flip into a slightly deranged, controlling and aggressive behaviour that is coming from their distress at being out of balance.

Secondly, a type may be operating in another type specifically in response to meeting someone. This would be an instinctive response to what the person picks up as attractive to the new potential mate. For example, a Lunar type may take advantage of the benevolent relationship he/she enjoys with the Saturn type (and become heavily intellectual) or go forward to Venus type (and appear to 'do everything from love'). They will continue to attempt to keep up this façade – until they simply run out of energy. Then they will revert to their essence type and again the other person will be confronted with a stranger. Depending on the other side, and their type, the relationship may be able to ride out and adapt to this abrupt change. Or it may not.

Finally, whenever we meet someone new we put on our best behaviour. The normally quiet become temporarily sparkling. The usually slothful find energy and run about the place for a while. But if we are not being true to our Enneagram type, we will eventually return to our essence type, at which point we may dig in our heels and say 'this is how I am and I'm not going to change'. That is why it is better to understand where we fit in the 12-type Enneagram, so as to ensure that we are not inadvertently setting ourselves up for relationship failure. It is infinitely better to know where we are on the Enneagram, and look for a mate *who appreciates and is nurtured by our essence-type energy*, rather than to go through a series of relationships where we are frustrated in our efforts to be what we are not.

Some Different Types in Love

A Lunar-type man and a Venus-type woman: He takes cover in childishness and she rages because her 'womanhood' is not being taken seriously. *The solution.* After an introduction to the 12-type Enneagram, the man learns to access both Venus- and Saturn-type energy, giving him the emotional key, plus the wisdom to know how to apply it. The woman learns to move from the still emotional centre of Venus type towards Mercury type and brings some energy of her own into the relationship, thus relieving the man of the pressure of having to do the work for both of them.

A Mars-type wife and a Jupiter-type husband: The arguments are always about what she sees as his 'wimpishness', while he finds her fire energy 'abrasive'.

The solution. The woman learns to move into Jupiter-type compassion for her gentle spouse. The husband learns not to fear her abrasive manner, appreciating that this is coming from her essence energy and he need not take it 'personally'. He instead understands the need for him to stand his ground and speak back clearly, logically and even forcefully, in a way his wife can deal with and respect. In other words he learns that in order to foster a happy relationship he must learn to operate positively in Mars type. Since this involves a *backwards move*, from Jupiter back to Mars type, this might seem retrogressive and in a sense it is. However, each type can fairly easily manifest the energy in the previous essence type and in this case it is for the right reasons.

A Mercury-type man and a Venus-type man: Their arguments centre on the Mercury type's desire to visit as many art galleries as possible, while the Venus type wants only to stay at home, cook and spend one-to-one time.

The solution. The couple learn to compromise on their very different operating speeds (72 beats and 144 beats). Venus types parcel out their energy carefully and do not like other people making demands on it. So instead the Venus type agrees to the Mercury type organizing *other* suitable companions for the various cultural visits. Although for some couples this division of interests might be fatal, especially since one of those suitable companions might also become a threat, the Venus type knows that, as is characteristic of the energy, the Mercury-type partner is just not that sexually motivated or bothered. So the arrangement is safe.

A Lunar-type woman and a Jupiter-type woman: Their confrontations revolve around the Jupiter type wanting to *smother* the Lunar type with loving gestures.

The solution. The Jupiter type learns to respect the freedom and independence so important to the Lunar type: she learns not to fill in everything for her partner, but allows her partner to dream and play her way into the same result. The Lunar type learns not to default into Mars type when reacting to her partner, but to move to Jupiter-type energy and support her partner's attempts to improve things.

A Lunar-type woman and a Venus–Mercury type man:
This couple is at loggerheads over the woman's lack of interest in household chores, and the man's seemingly reckless way of running his career.

The solution. Although we might stereotypically expect that the man always 'runs' the relationship, this is true with this couple only so far as the everyday organization and the overall emotional grounding of the relationship. Because the man's energy is fairly far from Saturn-type thinking, and the woman's intuitive grasp of matters is superior, the couple learn that complicated work matters – negotiating contracts and salary, dealing with backbiting – is best *formulated* by the woman, and *carried out* by the man. Similarly, in domestic issues, the man negotiates a housework schedule for the woman, who then obligingly carries it out because as a Lunar type she wants to make the 'adult' happy.

Recognizing Combinations that Work and that Don't
Two of the Same Type

Each type gets on with their own type because they recognize in the other something of themselves. However, this is not an instant, all-applicable answer because of *type limitations.*

Lunar with Lunar type: Both crave stability and emotional support. However, both are strongly independent and default to Mars type.

Venus type with Venus type: Both appreciate the other's interest in appearances and beauty. However, both are the still centre and expect the other to run around for them.

Mercury type with Mercury type: Both enjoy the other's knowledge of practical things and their ability to cover a lot of bases. However, both are broadly non-romantic.

Saturn type with Saturn type: Both appreciate each other's sense of questioning and prizing of worth. However, neither is emotional and both are anti-social and secretive.

Mars type with Mars type: Both appreciate the other's sense of adventure and boldness. However, both see relationships as competition and ownership.

Jupiter type with Jupiter type: Both prize the generosity and love they see in the other. However, both have complicated self-doubts and both may seek to compensate for these imagined faults by turning their attention on the other and not accepting what the other needs to offer themselves.

The Type Ahead

The most constructive relationship, from one individual's point of view, is a relationship which is conducted with a person *one type ahead*. Thus, when we consider that we overcome type limitations by progressing to the next type, being in a relationship with someone who *is* that type is an enormous help *for one of us*. For the other person it is less helpful because they have come from the previous type, and rather than being in that orbit, *they* benefit from moving towards the next type. However, if we have been exposed to the 12-type Enneagram, both can benefit from the relationship. The type ahead uses the security and support of the relationship to go towards their own next energy type. All these motivations and type aspects create some interesting combinations.

Venus type with Mercury type: The Venus type learns how to operate in Mercury-type energy, thus overcoming the stasis characteristic of Venus type. The Mercury type advances by moving towards Saturn type. So the Venus type also learns to operate two types ahead and learns to manifest Saturn type's deeper, slower thinking.

Jupiter type with Lunar type: The Jupiter type gains by experiencing and manifesting the self-focused, lighter Lunar-type energy. The Lunar type gains by moving towards Venus type. So the Jupiter type learns to adapt their style of loving all to loving one-to-one – thus enabling the Lunar type to experience Venus type manifestations of the Jupiter type.

Saturn–Mars hybrid type with Jupiter type: Because the hybrid type can already access Mars-type energy, the beneficial forward movement is best experienced with a Jupiter type. Having the Lunar-type default/relationship that is part of Saturn type, the Saturn–Mars hybrid manifests lighter Lunar-type energy in order to give their Jupiter-type partner some relief from their demands and responsibilities.

Less Beneficial Type Combinations

If someone had the ability to spend some time at the divorce courts and examine the affected couples from a 12-type Enneagram point of view, what unlucky or unworkable combinations would they be most likely to find?

Couples where the types are polar opposites may experience 'irreconcilable differences'. Lunar and Mars types; Venus and Saturn types. Of the hybrids, one of the younger hybrids such as the Lunar–Venus has difficulty with the physical or brain power of the older types. As well, the two type influences may cross The Divide: the diffident Jupiter–Lunar type may be impressed, or dismayed, by the Saturn–Mars type's strong sense of personal vision.

Couples where the dominant partner is the type behind the other. For example, a demanding Mercury type might wear out a Saturn type, particularly if the Mercury type will not respond to Saturn's need to educate or if the Saturn type decides the Mercury type is *unworthy* of their attention.

Couples where type limitations cannot be overcome. Two Mars types may make a power couple for a while, but they also make dangerous enemies for each other because each needs to be in control and dominant. Two Venus types may create an intense, over-sensitive, neurasthenic dynamic that is not healthy.

Couples where one or both are operating out of their essence type. A Mars type operating in Venus–Mercury hybrid type will be attractive to a Lunar type but this is not sustainable. A Jupiter type operating in Mercury type will attract a Venus type but once the Jupiter-type influence becomes predominant, the Venus type will resent coming second to their partner's other commitments.

This is a general guide that does not attempt to make individual cases into universal truths. It rather gives examples of how the wisdom of the 12-type Enneagram can be applied in our everyday circumstances. It is obvious that knowledge of the 12-type Enneagram can be highly beneficial in identifying appropriate mate-material. The system is also highly effective in being brought to bear on relationships that are already experiencing discord or internal stress. The diagram of the 12-type Enneagram, and the reality and application of the system, is infinitely useful. It needs only the specifics of a particular situation to begin the process of improving our relationships both to ourselves, and our potential or existing partners.

PART FOUR

Work and the Types

Chapter 10

The Enneagram at Work

Introduction: The Way it is *Without* the Enneagram

Without the benefit of the wisdom that we interpret from the 12-type Enneagram, our work life, as with the other aspects of our existence, may be nothing more than random incidents and chance encounters. People speak of 'falling into a job' or 'I'm doing this till something better comes along' or, worse, 'Me, I work *for my sins.*' Many of us regard our jobs as a 'necessary evil': those hours of the day when we become a robot, or a cog in a giant, unfeeling and uncaring wheel. The idea of *rewarding work* may be reserved for those occupations we engage in voluntarily *outside* of business hours.

Each type has its own particular attitude to 'work' as a concept. For some types it is a tiresome burden; for others work is the most satisfying way to experience and express who they are. Realistically, since for most of us there is an obligation to perform some sort of gainful employment, by applying the idea that we have all the essence type-energies within us, we can more consciously access the correct type-energy for overcoming whatever may be holding us back: our essence type's passivity, resistance, fearfulness or lack of ability.

The different ways each type's essence energy manifests lead to distinct and identifiable patterns of work life. We can readily imagine that some types will do better in the work arena than others. The younger types, particularly the Lunar, Lunar–Venus and Venus types, struggle to find somewhere to fit into the 'adult' world of work. Venus–Mercury, Mercury and Mercury–Saturn types are valued for their speed and their prolific output. There are types who regard work as an opportunity to understand themselves and others better (Saturn and Saturn–Mars types), or to exert the power they find so important (Mars type). Two of the 12 types view work as their salvation: through working they may consciously or unconsciously seek to 'redeem' themselves and ultimately pay back for the gift of life, the gift of which they often feel unworthy (Mars–Jupiter; Jupiter types). The last type works with dedication and with admirable responsibility although they sometimes yearn for a different sort of life, in which *they* are looked after (Jupiter–Lunar type).

Type Understanding for the Right Career

Although it is true that we can learn to consciously access any of the type-energies, and benefit from these different type-energies, we must also be aware of the potential drawbacks and dangers of operating for long periods of time *out* of our essence type. Each energy feeds in a particular way and by being out of our essence type for long periods we are literally starving ourselves of energy nourishment. In the long term it may cause the individual less grief to accept that some areas of work are *better* closed to us because our essence type finds it so difficult to support the unsuitable ongoing mental, emotional and physical demands.

Lunar types, for example, may take some particular thing they enjoy, such as the fun of serving drinks and food to their friends, and enrol on a food and beverage degree course, where they become overwhelmed by management, finance and other technical requirements that may be beyond them, but ideal for Mars types. Mars types may be attracted to 'fun' working environments, but find their direct, blunt energy out of step with the bubbly, more dream-creative Lunar-type energy. Languorous Venus types in busy offices need to learn either to step up to Mercury-type speed, or to take a less demanding position where they are not staying late to finish the workload. So we can readily see that learning about the Enneagram will save much distress and an eventual sense of failure in our work lives.

All types have their own dreams, illusions, work ideals and ideas and to achieve our goals we need one of two things. The first is the good fortune to be born in an essence type to which that ideal form of activity comes relatively naturally (someone dreams of being a doctor and opening new medical territories; they are a Mars–Jupiter type, so the dream and the type enjoy a high level of congruence). The second path is to learn first about the 12-type Enneagram and then develop a way of working which more consciously acknowledges the limitations of your own type-energy, and learns how best to apply the appropriate energies available from other types.

Overcoming Essence Type Limitations

While repeating the warning that it is not a good idea to choose a career that is not ultimately supported by your essence energy, working in a career more consciously is the way we *may* be able to overcome and live with our type shortcomings.

For example, a developed Lunar type, who can see that there is more to a degree course than serving drinks to their parents' friends, in selecting a four-year food and beverage degree course consciously *anticipates* the problems he or she will encounter by first taking additional courses that will bring them more up to technical speed. The Lunar type knows that they are not good at maths, or managing groups of people, so they focus on these areas and by learning how to access the other type-energies – Mercury–Saturn type for bettering their maths; Mars type for managing groups (in a conscious default) – they thus acquire enough for their purpose. You don't have to be the best at every aspect of a job: shine in your strong points (Lunar types make charming restaurant hosts) and find ways to support your weak points (don't fall into the Lunar-type blindness trap of believing you have to do everything yourself, which is a wrong manifestation of 'independence': get outside help).

Similarly, a Saturn-type person who wants a career in fashion will struggle, at least at the beginning, because the *atmosphere* will involve more Venus-type energy. They must learn to 'feel' the purpose of the business rather than questioning and judging it on its 'merits' or 'worth'. The disadvantage should fade as the person climbs the career ladder. At some point their Saturn-type advantages will come into play, and they may become, for example, *commentators* on fashion, able to cross-reference designers' influences and relate one fashion trend to another to their hearts' and minds' content. Different 12-type Enneagram types are drawn to each industry; just as each type views life differently, so each finds its own form of expression.

A Curious Work Phenomenon

People often have a curious relationship to their jobs. Where people are genuinely struggling, it is helpful to consider if the job suits their essence type. But where people are good at their jobs, but believe they are not, or that they are phonies and about to be found out, something else is going on. The individual may be a younger type, or a hybrid spanning The Divide (Mercury–Saturn and Jupiter–Lunar types). They access the older energy in actually producing the work, but judge themselves negatively from the more vulnerable, younger energy. How we approach this can be the difference between eventual success or failure. In order to bridge the gap, individuals may turn to some form of addiction. The City of London (the business sector) is known to be rife with financial types who drive themselves on with a combination of cocaine and tranquillizers – rather than turning *inward* for what they are lacking. 'Getting out of my head' at the end of the day will not prepare you as well for the next day as doing something *emotionally nourishing* (in other words, rather than ending the day in Mars/Lunar-type irresponsibility, consciously choose to nurture yourself with Venus-type energy).

It is also essential, after we have demanded that our bodies and our emotions work for us, to take a moment to acknowledge that they have done their job. We need to say to ourselves 'well done', to fill our bodies with Venus-type love and Jupiter-type fulfilment. If we don't give ourselves what we need, we tend to *reward ourselves externally* – so that may be with drugs, gambling, alcohol misuse or the wrong kind of sex, or some other addictive hit which, rather than really accomplishing the purpose, merely moves us just another degree away from a sense of inner balance. Finally, it is also important that after we have been to Jupiter-type energy we begin again with Lunar-type energy so that we start a new work cycle *with enthusiasm*. Otherwise we may burn out, since each cycle, rather than starting with new energy, is riding off the back of the exhausted energy left over from the previous one.

Business Benefits to Working with the Enneagram

There are multiple benefits, which we can divide into three categories:

- By understanding our own type, we see where we fit in, and where we are more likely to struggle.
- By understanding the types of our co-workers, subordinates and bosses, we increase our ability to work with them.
- For management. By understanding the types, we choose people fit for the task: we bring together the right blend of types and avoid predictable clashes and disappointments.

Understanding Ourselves

These observations are a general guide. A number of factors, such as coming into a family business, or the basic lack of other jobs, result in people being in situations that are not really supported by their type-energies.

Lunar type

More Appropriate: Work that gives the type the opportunity to engage with others, but also leaves them enough time to return to their own inner world, where they 'dream' and make connections and play creatively. The current upsurge of consultant or freelance working patterns well suits this type because they can be 'professional' and 'adult' for some time, and then have the space they need to replenish their childlike energy, by dreaming a personal reality into existence.
Less Appropriate: Relentless work and constant deadlines. Multiple, shifting priorities and work for a number of different bosses. Any job that requires constant attention to detail and organization.

Lunar–Venus type

More Appropriate: Remembering that this hybrid type is between the intuitive knowledge of Lunar type, and the grounded physical presence of Venus type, Lunar–Venus type is often found in temporary work situations and places where their combination doesn't count against them – take-away servers, estate agents, nannies, actors, small-scale entrepreneurs.

Less Appropriate: Anything too 'grown up' in terms of responsibility or where there is too much riding on *them* personally.

Venus type

More Appropriate: Jobs that require good personal presentation. Jobs in glamorous professions. Because the type functions fairly slowly, jobs where the personal touch or schmoozing is appreciated – beauty and tanning salons, clothes shops and gyms (this is why personal trainers talk about their personal lives) – are desirable. Since the type prefers one-to-one relationships, working for a single boss is appealing.
Less Appropriate: Work where technical achievements are more important than presenting a warm and glamorous presence. Working to constant pressure and deadlines.

Venus–Mercury type

More Appropriate: With the joint influences of emotion and speed, this type looks for employment in fields where they can work with people. However, this type can surprise, so could also be found in seemingly atypical jobs, such as accountancy, because of their ability to deal with detail.
Less Appropriate: Speeding away from Mars-type energy influence, they have a tendency to avoid confrontation and work discord. Being 'fun-loving' they often have a strong need to be liked by everyone. Therefore not recommended for jobs where making tough decisions, particularly ones with personnel complications, are a regular feature.

Mercury type

More Appropriate: Jobs where their organizational skills and speed are appreciated. Co-ordinating different priorities and dealing with different personalities is welcomed by this type. Positions where they can use their extensive contacts and knowledge of computers/politics/night life are also a plus.
Less Appropriate: Too great a management role or a job where thinking globally and at depth is a constant requirement.

Mercury–Saturn type

More Appropriate: With the speed of Mercury type and going towards the deep-thinking Saturn type, this type is successful in creative and organizational spheres.

Less Appropriate: The triumph of speed over thought may mean a high creative output that is enormously variable in terms of quality. For example, a prolific film-maker of this hybrid type will have some work which has depth as well as commercial success, but also some stunningly shallow work, whereas a Saturn-type film maker would be more likely to release fewer, but more rewarding, pictures.

Saturn type

More Appropriate: Work which dovetails with their attention to depth and their natural fascination with questioning and connecting. Will willingly take responsibility for conceptual and academic input.

Less Appropriate: Jobs involving feelings, such as 'mine host' restaurant owner, or work which needs to be done without question, such as carrying out military instructions. Saturn types will also find jobs with ongoing confrontation difficult, especially with Mars types, who are operating faster than them and will tie them in verbal knots.

Saturn–Mars type

More Appropriate: We remember that this type draws other people to them. They often have a belief that chimes in with the *Zeitgeist* of the time, or they have a knack for reading the mood. Therefore work would be looking towards visionary or global impact. Well suited to CEO roles.

Less Appropriate: Work that has one-to-one limits, such as tutoring individual pupils. Work where they cannot express their strength and leadership.

Mars type

More Appropriate: Management and authority are appealing concepts to this type, who rise up the ladder by over-performing until they reach a level satisfactory to themselves.

Less Appropriate: Low-status positions. Jobs without a hierarchical structure. Working towards goals impossible to define.

Mars–Jupiter type

More Appropriate: Jobs with a global or universal application. In business they thrive on 'green' concerns, and they are deeply committed to working ethically. This hybrid type will found charities single-handedly, driven by their deep passion and enormous energy.

Less Appropriate: Situations where they are unable to use their true talents and qualities. Stuck in the mundane or being in situations where they do not respect what they are doing.

Jupiter type

More Appropriate: Jobs where their caring and containing can be used. They prefer situations of authority where they can use reconciliation, compassion and humour rather than force.

Less Appropriate: Too much emphasis on personal self-development. Jobs where they must ruthlessly cut down staff numbers or deny services to those who need them.

Jupiter–Lunar type

More Appropriate: This hybrid type's combination of mature adult and childlike adult leads them towards work in which they can share their 'magical' type essence: adults working with children, or looking after a family or younger siblings. However they are not 'ditzy': Jupiter-type influence gives them presence and power. May be in high management positions where they become known for reliability and honesty in their work dealings. However, they can make and carry out tough measures with Mars-type ruthlessness and practicality, since they have come from that energy type.

Less Appropriate: May take on too many nurturing, mentoring relationships, while craving and not receiving the same support for themselves.

Understanding Colleagues

Here we see how different types are best used at work:

Lunar types

We would find this type helpful if we are brainstorming, particularly if we can take the raw input of Lunar-type intuition and, if we are Saturn type or are consciously accessing this type-energy, use it as the starting point for a deeper think-through. Lunar types can also be helpful because they don't get bogged down in daily routine; they come in each day with positive energy and because they are so much in their own inner world, they don't ask 'big' questions (they may innocently ask an awkward question but because they *don't appreciate the seriousness of it* they don't pursue it, as would a Saturn or Mars type).

Lunar–Venus types

Again, creative, but more earthy, less intuitive. Their fondness for fooling around in a sexual way may make for a stimulating environment in which people feel 'turned on', more aware of themselves physically, which would bring a more stimulating energy to their work.

Venus types

Good listeners, sympathetic and genuinely interested. Will keep the office looking its best.

Venus–Mercury types

Their place of work will either be meticulous or a mess of piled papers, depending on which influence prevails. Good relationship workers known for being 'nice'. Can, on specific issues, often make the jump to Saturn-type depth, although they can also be surprisingly naïve since they are moving towards speed and away from Venus-type energy's earth rooting (they may not recognize danger at work since they are not naturally suspicious). They may make business decisions based on speed rather than thinking through the various elements.

Mercury types

Essential for co-ordinating, organizing, delivering. Work best in supportive and middle-management positions where their possible lack of focus in pursuing a project to a finish is not a drawback.

Mercury–Saturn types

Popular for the speedy work turn-arounds they achieve as well as contributing some depth of thinking. Work documents may then need a deeper analysis. Unlike the other young types, because this one has both 'younger' and 'older' influences they will ask for help rather than go under.

Saturn types

Their brainpower makes them highly desirable. Given that their operating rate is only 80 beats a minute they are happier in research, less happy as the front-line spokesperson.

Saturn–Mars types

Good at projects they can personally run and shine in. Good when they are in charge. Will build high brand-recognition with themselves at the centre.

Mars types

Operational and functional. As has been a theme in this book, we remember that the Mars-type energy is essential for business and work management. There may be difficulties inherent in working *with* this type, since they will, whenever possible and they're not stopped, read 'with' as 'under' and create a hierarchy with themselves at the top even with co-workers on the same level.

Mars–Jupiter types

Tend to find work that suits their enormous energy and interest in bettering some aspect of humanity. Able to work under great pressure, with few resources. May become easily bored if the work is not challenging enough or they deem it beneath their line of what is worthwhile so that they may be lost to another 'more worthy' company.

Jupiter types

Crises that disturb other types are approached with a laugh, which helps to put the situation in perspective. Will often be responsible for the *tone* of the office or work environment in that other types will look to the Jupiter type for guidance and approval, particularly if the Jupiter type is in charge. Are not bothered by – in fact they seek out – projects that have little chance of fully succeeding, like World Peace or Ending World Poverty.

Jupiter–Lunar types

Excellent managers and supportive of staff. However, because they have the energy influences of both mature adult and childlike adult, they may sometimes be surprisingly vulnerable and their 'child' energy may emerge in the naivety of some of their thinking, or the way they speak. They appreciate thoughtful comments that validate their work and themselves, although seeming to brush these off (they savour them later, on their own).

Understanding People Who Work for You

From a management perspective, these are suggestions for how employers should recruit, and work with, the different types:

Lunar types

The 'creatives'. Often management will have the sense to leave this type alone so they can 'dream' up whatever is necessary, using Lunar-type intuition, fantasy and imagination. For example, a market analyst will be left to 'play' with the morning's newspapers or to go for a walk while his or her mind makes sense of the various fragments and puts them into a work strategy (the analyst may in fact be a Saturn type, but they will still begin from Lunar-type energy because the intuitive nature of the energy facilitates original thinking and connection-making).

Lunar–Venus types

Again, creative and enthusiastic. Management may not appreciate the difference between this hybrid and the one before them, and force the type into a regimented, non-sexy way of being at work that could make the type feel confused and possibly shamed. This type works best when they are accepted entirely as they present themselves and loved for what they are. They will reject management's ambitions for them since, even if they put on a good show, they inwardly suspect they lack the particular resilience necessary.

Venus types

The well-groomed face of the work environment. The person or people who check that the plants are watered, the office clean and that people are feeling comfortable. As a manager, be aware that the Venus type will have difficulty answering other people's phones or 'pitching in' when you are short-staffed. They aren't lazy, but anything outside what they see as their own area of responsibility is a major effort for them.

Venus–Mercury types

The combination of emotional detail and volume (speed-based) means this type needs not so much management as appreciation (with the influence of both Venus and Mercury types, this hybrid type *loves* being appreciated and will remember and repeat any favourable feedback: management benefits from remembering this).

Mercury types

The 144-beats-a-minute energy is vital for coping in a fast-paced work environment. Care needs to be taken, though, in ensuring that the Mercury type does not lose sight of their own needs. It should be remembered that the Mercury type, as with the other types already listed in this category, is a *younger* type, and management may need to give them more face-time than *older* types. A problem in business is that the Mercury type's speed causes them to shine easily, so they get more responsibility, which management needs to understand the type may not be grounded enough to deliver.

Mercury–Saturn types

Because speed often overrides depth with this hybrid type, particularly when they are undeveloped, management needs to be aware that their first draft will not be the best, and allow them time really to engage with the issue/project.

Saturn types

Can without question be trusted to run with work. Giving them deadlines may be necessary because of Saturn type's unending questioning and research orientation.

Saturn–Mars types

This type's 'back-off: I know what I'm doing' attitude to management requires that supervision be given with a light hand. This type is most often discovered at partner and management level.

Mars types

Managing Mars-type energy is a delicate operation. A combination of allowing the type control, together with ensuring the Mars type is clear who is the boss, works best. Mars types in a subordinate role will tend to yield loyally to higher authority. However, they may be autocratic with their own reportees. This may require a Jupiter-type benevolent overseeing from the higher authority, to rein them in.

Mars–Jupiter types

Since this type will most probably be in a management position, any management input will be on an equal level. They will tell you what they are doing out of politeness rather than because they need permission. You may also find this type quietly filling a fairly menial position.

Jupiter types

This type's range runs from the person who does the photo-copying to the chairman of the board (but the photocopier will organize all the leaving cards and with this type the chairman's door is always open for staff concerns). Jupiter types learn not to expect that their love and concern will be acknowledged, but a wise manager will ensure that they get personal recognition; even if the Jupiter type will brush it off, inside they are pleased to be seen to be of value.

Jupiter–Lunar types

This hybrid type can also be trusted with whatever the job is. However, since they can become confused in Lunar-type need, or take on too much personal responsibility, which is then in conflict with their Lunar-type need for independence and space, they may need management time to talk through their workload.

Although these brief delineations focus on an office environment, this in no way limits the influences of the 12-type Enneagram to such a formal style of workplace:

- A street-sweeper may be distinguished by the deep conversations they enjoy with local residents. This could indicate a Saturn type.
- The man who delivers groceries may take great care in avoiding your ornaments and comment on your décor. This could indicate a Venus type.
- The woman who sells you cigarettes may point out the health warning. This could indicate a Jupiter type.
- The woman behind the counter at the garage may be co-ordinating administration tasks while she runs your credit card through the machine. This could indicate a Mercury type.
- Your personal trainer may enjoy spinning elaborate fantasies while watching you work out. This could indicate a Lunar type.
- You may be surprised to learn from a PA that all the partners are 'dead scared of me'. She will say this with grim, deep satisfaction. This would indicate a Mars type.

Why You Might Benefit from Changing Career Path

This section is intended only to be helpful. If you are satisfied with your career path, and your 12-type Enneagram profile is sufficiently matched to your own satisfaction, then it is not necessary to consider a change.

However, if you have struggled, or are currently struggling, in your present situation, discovering how you can apply the wisdom of the 12-type Enneagram will aid you in making a more informed decision. Granted, this world does not often present us with a variety of options all tailored entirely to suit us, but by becoming *conscious* of who you are in terms of your essence type, and thinking about jobs or work environments from the perspective of what is *more* helpful or *less* helpful, you at least give yourself an insight into why you may struggle more than some other people to accomplish work tasks.

For example, a Lunar type (operating at 96 beats a minute) who finds employment as a personal assistant can cope with the Mercury-type environment (144 beats a minute) for some time, but will become tired out, and need space and quiet to recharge, while the Mercury type just keeps going. Even if the Lunar type cannot change their job to one that better suits, at least understanding *why* they sometimes struggle stops them from becoming too discouraged. Ideally, a manager will realize when they have a Lunar type on their hands and may be able to move them to a more suitable position.

Likewise, a Mars-type person in a lowly post with a single reportee may become a tyrant to that one person. It is better – at least for the reportee – if the reportee is assigned to someone else, and the Mars type is given authority over something that does not include responsibility for another member of staff. Of course, a Mars type put in charge of the stationery cupboard will become a tyrant here as well, so again, their thirst for control needs to be carefully matched to work needs so as not to create an inappropriate power base.

But when we consider *you*, the reader, we can ask a few probing questions:

- What are the work conversations you like to have?
- At the end of the day, what makes you feel satisfied?
- Who are the people you admire, or envy, in terms of how they spend their working day?
- What ability do you believe you may have to find this satisfaction for yourself?
- What are you prepared to sacrifice, if necessary, to achieve your better working conditions or environment?

Process? What's that?

The rise of reality television and some of the current talent shows has done away with the concept of *process*. No longer do people see their working life beginning with a long apprenticeship. Nowadays a typical goal seems to be instant wild fame and recognition. However, this remains a fantasy for most of us. We still need to learn how to acquire something through a cycle of effort. By considering the six main-type energies in the 12-type Enneagram, we become more conscious of the cycle of this process:

> **Lunar-type energy:** Here we *dream* what a better job would look like. We *imagine* how our life would be improved.
>
> **Venus-type energy:** Here we find the *passion* that gives us energy for the task ahead.
>
> **Mercury-type energy:** Here we put into place the practical issues. We send off letters, research on the Internet, network and *create the opportunity* for ourselves.
>
> **Saturn-type energy:** Here we consider deeply both the reality of the work we wish to take on, and also how this will work with the rest of our lives. It will not work if we decide to become a principal ballet dancer at forty. However, we may become a model at sixty if our face has aged in an interesting way, or we may become a teacher at fifty if we can work our way into it. In Saturn type we *question* and consider *how realistic* our goal is.
>
> **Mars-type energy:** Assuming we have done our homework and our concept has some realistic chance of success, here we *market* ourselves. We *make* the opportunities we need; we find the openings that we had not realized existed. We use boldness and confidence and we do not give up till we have succeeded.
>
> **Jupiter-type energy:** Here we realize the value of not always being in pursuit of our goal, but having enough to be satisfied. Here we include others, and widen the perspective beyond ourselves so we can assess the value, worth and impact of our contribution. Finally we cherish ourselves for the effort we have made, regardless of its success in the Outerworld.

The last, Jupiter-type stage is one that may elude some if

their goal is more to do with making money than having their work life reflect something of greater worth. This means that the cycle stops at Mars-type energy, rather than completing in Jupiter-type energy. It is better to avoid terminating work plans in Mars-type energy because this robs the world of *getting something back*. Someone who is interested in the ideas of the 12-type Enneagram will soon discover that finishing a work goal in Mars-type energy is unsatisfactory.

This is why we often see that people who have achieved in a business capacity will become major supporters of particular charities, or fund some sort of enterprise. In fact, the business person who has made their own way up in the world and has now established a fund or mentorship is a modern cliché – although a far more valuable one than some other clichés. Although the actual work they do may still terminate in Mars-type energy, they are still actualizing Jupiter-type energy by using the money thus acquired for the good of others.

PART FIVE

Further Investigations into the 12-Type Enneagram

Chapter 11

General Notes on Where We Are

Imagine you are reading the morning paper. Tragic life stories and images of violence, a film actor attends his latest premiere, the government is criticized for going back on promises. You turn the page and are suddenly confronted with an image of stars in space, a photo taken with a sophisticated telescope of 'a collision between two galaxies with a supermassive black hole at its heart . . . twelve million light years away'. For a moment you recognize that the troubles and triumphs of this world, and those in our own lives, are lived out on one planet, in this one moment in time, in one solar system among many, many others. At points like this we experience a shift in perception in which our own circumstances melt away in the face of the virtually unknown and endless enormity of which we are an infinitesimal part. Then we have to go on with our day because although on a cosmic level our needs and wants are irrelevant, they are nevertheless real, present and important to us.

In reading and thinking over the information available to us through the 12-type Enneagram we are helped if we can deepen and widen our appreciation of all the circumstances that make up what we think of as our life. We can think about ourselves and those we know in terms of how to use the wisdom of this cosmology to understand who we truly are, how the invisible and hitherto unknown cosmic influences that affect us are operating, and how to gain from our understanding. Regarding our relationship to other people, we can ponder on how we can deepen and clarify our understanding of type energies by observing their manifestation in the words and actions of those around us. This is not the same as telling someone to 'do' something or 'not do' something else: whenever we use the information of the 12-type Enneagram it is important to treat the knowledge, and the person we are working with, with respect.

Let us consider more deeply the implications and applications of the meaning and consequences of the alchemical effect of the planetary energy forces on us.

One principal aim in studying the 12-type Enneagram is to learn as much as possible about our motivations. These motivations arise both from our essence type-energy, and also from our unconscious moving around the other energies in the diagram. We wish to make our journey more *conscious*, more under our choice and control, rather than merely being led by the various type-energies to 'act out' the particularities of our own and other types.

Part of our motivations come from our assumptions. It is not possible to understand *just how unconscious and mechanical* is our behaviour, and how that behaviour is tied to our essence type – fundamentally it is *the expression of our essence type*. Although we may, in the course of a day, access some or most of the other essence energies, we are still deeply immersed in our essence type-energy. Therefore, for example, the Lunar type has no idea how 'Lunar-intoxicated' he or she is: Saturn types do not understand how 'Saturn-bound' they are. We must not believe that, because we are accessing other energies, we are a split type, capable of functioning equally in two diverse types. For example, someone may state 'I am a Lunar type, but I'm also a Mars type'; they are simply describing how they go to *the wrong type-influence* when they default.

For hybrid types, there is not, for example, one Saturn–Mars type force that belongs to the Saturn-type side, and another Saturn–Mars force that belongs to the Mars-type side. It is an *ever-changing reality* that partakes more of whatever main type it is closest to. All the time the type is getting *intermingling type-force influences*.

Major-Cycle Influences

These take place over our lifetime when, during this particular life, we are most influenced by our situation. We may be either directly on a type point (a main type, numbers 1, 4, 2, 8, 5, 7) or somewhere between that point and the next point in the series (a hybrid type). We are, in this larger respect, *on a one-point journey around the 12-type Enneagram*. At a major-cycle level we move *only slightly* during our lifetime and we are influenced by our more or less static placement on the 'large path' – the numbers 1, 4, 2, 8, 5, 7. Looking at the situation from this large perspective, our BeingSelf is travelling very slowly. We can be 'tracked' as being somewhere between one sign and the next sign on the chart. One Lunar type may be closest to the Lunar-type centre; another person, also a Lunar type, would principally be somewhere on the line between Lunar type and Venus type, or could be out of essence type and somewhere between Lunar type and Mercury type.

There are literally an *infinite number of places* a person can be on that line. It is a *continuum of possibility*. However, for our lifetime, to the greatest extent we stay put *wherever on the line we are*. Therefore, the idea that, if we become aware of the 12-type Enneagram, we can then 'choose' our energy type is wrong. We must be honest and have a sense of humility about where we are, and work to increase our understanding both of the nature of that place, and what we need to move towards the next type (while remembering that although we will gain from this conscious acquisition, this does not change our overall placement in terms of our major-cycle influences).

Forwards? Backwards?

As noted earlier, the Enneagram lines connect two entities but we must learn always to travel in the correct direction – 1, 4, 2, 8, 5, 7 – and back to 1. Lunar type and Venus type are connected. But if a Venus type goes backwards to Lunar type and tries to be intuitive in a Venus-type interpretation of a mental process, it is a disaster because the Venus type will act stupidly and imagine that it is the right thing to do. Both entities are compromised. Lunar type imagining 'love' nonsense coming towards it from Venus type (wrong direction), gets stupefied and is shaken out of their Discrimination Mind setting. The Discrimination Mind setting is different for each of the energies. It is the proper functioning of each type. For Lunar type it is correctly using intuition.

Another example is when Saturn type goes backwards towards Mercury type. This happens when either the Saturn type, or someone with influence, values speed over depth. The Saturn type will become dismayed and dissatisfied with multiple tasks given a surface treatment and they also become shaken out of their Discrimination Mind setting. For Saturn types this results in a loss in the value they place on their intellectual facility.

Possibility of Changing Essence Type

People often *imagine* that they have changed their essence type. Even when work or personal circumstances force or benefit an individual to operate in a different type-energy, they will find that after a while the unnatural energy drains them. Whereas a Mars type will be 'fed' by bold energy, a Lunar, Mercury or other type wanting to exploit the confidence/aggression of Mars type will burn out over time. So changing essence type is not a goal. Our work is concerned with understanding our own essence type and where we go to temporarily for other support.

Journeys through the Enneagram from Each Type

You are now familiar with the idea that if we divide '1' into '7' we achieve the number .142857. It bears repeating that, as was noted in Chapter 1, there is a further secret within this series of numbers. If we multiply the string of numbers, we achieve the *same progression of numbers* up till the multiplication by 6:

$$1 \div 7 = .142857$$
$$2 \times .142857 = .285714$$
$$3 \times .142857 = .428571$$
$$4 \times .142857 = .571428$$
$$5 \times .142857 = .714285$$
$$6 \times .142857 = .857142$$

However, when we multiply the number .142857 by 7 we achieve .999999. This does not progress anywhere. Thus we work only with six numbers, and six main types. Please review Chapter 1 for more on the meaning of this phenomenon.

This Life? Next Life?

The idea that we move within the same major-cycle influence *in this life* is obviously of enormous interest, given that it completely reverses some of the expectations of, for example, basic Christian thought which maintains that once we die we go to 'heaven' or 'hell'. It reinforces the ideas of those who follow some form of reincarnation. However, pinning down these speculations is outside the purpose of this book. Instead, let us continue to map cycle influences.

Mini-Cycle Influences

Although we are in this static place, we *travel in a minor way*, around the numbers 1, 4, 2, 8, 5, 7 path many times an hour/a day/a week/a year. As noted previously, we bounce *unconsciously* round the types. Therefore we move in a chaotic way. Let us again take something we all do – wake up in the morning and face life – and see this as an appropriate progress of the different type-energies:

We wake in the morning. We all begin in the Dreamworld (Lunar-type energy) and as we wake up, our mind moves to Venus type (how do I feel/what do I feel like doing/what will I wear?). Then we move towards the Mercury ray influence, where we prepare our physical selves for the day – shower, dress, eat, identify/remember what we have to do. At this point the three types on the 'younger' or 'lighter' side (Lunar, Venus, Mercury) *stop their volitional journey, and then deal with whatever comes up.*

But for *growth*, one would consciously go to the influence of the Saturn-type ray, to see what we could do on that particular day that would generate *a deeper meaning* for our lives. Then we would go to Mars-type energy, which would push us actually *to do* something. Then to Jupiter type to feel the satisfaction of having completed the cycle. We also need to bear in mind that in this way any of the types can move in a conscious way through the whole numbers 1, 4, 2, 8, 5, 7 journey yet, with all this, our major-cycle type sign usually remains the same. People imagine they 'change greatly', but generally they don't: Beethoven's compositions changed, but he remained mostly the same.

Beginning Your Individual Journey

Although most journeys as described in this book begin with number '1', it should not be understood that, whatever type you are, *you must begin with '1'*. This is the reason why we multiply numbers 1, 4, 2, 8, 5, 7 by 2, 3, 4, 5 and 6. Thus someone who is a Mercury type, starting a journey, would access the different type-energies in the following combination: numbers 2, 8, 5, 7, 1, 4. Someone who is a Saturn–Mars type's journey would be taken as numbers 8, 5, 7, 1, 4, 2, and similarly for other types.

There are two items of interest here:

1. The fascinating fact that the sequence of numbers remains the same whether multiplied by 2, 3, 4, 5, or 6.
2. The number sequence *always* sets out the correct path through the Enneagram. There is always only one path for correct development.

Nature/Nurture

This is a significant factor, with a quantifiable individual set of influences, either positive or negative. However, we must remember that most people have much less control over their lives than they imagine they have. Reality TV gives us abundant examples of people whose circumstances and talents in no way meet their ambitious and sometimes bizarre 'dreams'.

Yet we are not mere puppets; we can make meaningful choices in how we respond to or do not respond to the circumstances and influences in which we find ourselves. Take, for example, a person with a background disadvantaged both financially and with regard to family structure and security. If they are a Mars type, *given their type particularities,* they will still attempt to 'rise to the top' in whatever form is possible. It might be as the head of an illegal drug racket. A Mars–Jupiter type, similarly disadvantaged, might become a social worker or work with treating drug addiction. Thus each makes use of *their circumstances and essence influences,* but does not move too far away from the energy of their essence type.

Another example would be two Venus types: one, from a privileged background, schooled in being a gracious and glamorous hostess, makes a financially secure marriage. The other uses her interest in 'beauty' to become a hairdresser and spends her days in an atmosphere which suits her type characteristics. Both may believe they have 'forged their destiny' while not appreciating that their destiny was heavily influenced, if not entirely predicted, by their essence type.

Volition

The drive or movement aspect of forging one's life can also make the difference between happiness and fulfilment, or confusion, bitterness and failure. Let us examine two Lunar types:

The first has difficulties to overcome in the early years. It is *volition*, which we could also think of in terms of drive, which helps. By accessing the faster speed of Mercury type, the Lunar type learns to overcome his problems by quickly dropping what is not helping (Lunar-type energy is where we go to drop something), and concentrating (with the influence of some Mars-type thought) on what will produce the desired result. He learns to swallow disappointment (more Mars energy for resilience), replacing one disappointment with the hope of a new departure or possibility (Saturn-type philosophic stance/ Lunar-type hope). Most of all, he learns not to dwell on what has not worked out (which is negative Venus-type energy) and with each setback becomes more determined to be heard, to be noticed and appreciated (Saturn–Mars-type energy).

The second Lunar type has a relatively easy upbringing, so it is with a shock that he finds himself in adulthood. Faced with societal pressure to marry, he finds a mate who is 12-type Enneagram unsuitable (a Mars type), and marries. Where with *volition* he could overcome the difficulties endemic in the match, he slides into *inactivity* and avoidance. Each episode, each mini-crisis, could be resolved by a combination of volition and deep thinking, but he deals only with the moment and in this he constantly accedes to the demands of his spouse.

We see here one reason why we all need volition to overcome difficulties. This is one reason why Mars and Mercury types believe that just by *doing* the problem will be solved. For example, by giving someone money, or signing as a guarantor, that will suffice, 'just throwing money at the problem'. But unless Saturn-type energy is also involved, just doing may be the wrong thing (signing as a guarantor creates a hostage to fortune; reckless use of money avails nothing).

12-type Enneagram Study is a way towards making the most of *where-we-are* and *where-we-could-be-going*. It is comparable to the Aristotelian concept of *being* and *becoming*, which is also an aspect of 12-type Enneagram study.

Intermingled Time Sequences

We need to understand that the journey round the 12-type Enneagram types in the numbers 1, 4, 2, 8, 5, 7 sequence as well as the unconscious, chaotic way we habitually bounce round the various type-energies, does not happen individually and sequentially. On the contrary, *there are multiple journeys going on at the same time.* For example, we may be at the start of a personal relationship (Lunar and Venus-type energy) while at work we are completing a complex project (Mercury, Mars and eventually Jupiter-type energy). The different journeys have many short and long cycles. They happen interactively and simultaneously.

Caring for the 12-Type Enneagram

All these aspects deepen and strengthen our developing understanding of the 12-type Enneagram. Here we also see why it is extremely important that we do not 'use' the types as some form of party trick. Since the Enneagram holds the key both to understanding truly where we are and how we can develop, it should only be used with respect and responsibility. Understanding where we and others are in terms of the 12-type Enneagram is a significant and valuable addition to other knowledge we have already acquired. With it comes the responsibility that we will not use a fleeting, surface knowledge of a few words and phrases to give the impression that we are more knowledgeable than we actually are (see the final chapter of this book on avoiding being an 'instant expert').

Used with understanding and care the 12-type Enneagram opens up many possibilities for living our lives with more meaning. We should not dip in and out, picking the bits we can relate to other things that we know; *the keys can be given to us only up to the point to which we are pre-prepared and able to receive them.* This is the meaning of the curious biblical reference 'to him that has, more shall be given: to him who has only a little, even this will be taken away from him'. This does not mean that the cosmos punishes people who don't have much money: money is not a benchmark of worth or level of being. But if we have only a slight impression of the 12-type Enneagram, if we take one tiny fact and think that is enough, then the help we *could* get from the knowledge is lost because inside us there is nothing for it to hold onto. Gurdjieff talked of the 'magnetic centre'. This is the aspect of our psyche that can recognize something of real worth to us. The magnetic centre draws the nourishing information into our psyche. But then it fades away and we need something deeper inside us to carry on our interests. This is the phenomenon known to us in 'fads' or 'gimmicks'.

Overall, working in a small, real way, just for today, is better than attempting to take on a global 'cosmology' approach. We always gain from being simple and respectful. We always lose by confusing ourselves.

This Life and the Next

As previously stated, this cosmology is sympathetic to the concept that *in this life* we are in a particular type, and in the next, the next essence type. However, this is not a straightforward statement, and we must be careful that the implications of such an idea do not swamp us in irrelevant or pointless distractions from our purpose in *this* life.

We need to concentrate on this life: think about and work on what will and can happen in this life. Our purpose here is to work to be a *healthy representation of our home type*, to grow from:

- The first stage, in which we experience consciously having to deal with the characteristic flaws of our type, to:
- The second stage, in which we experience knowing much more about our type influences (in the form of 'planetary rays'), and try to work with the solid good characteristics of the type, to:

- The third stage, in which we reach out to all the aspects of *other* type characteristics in us, as a preparatory 'smoothing out' of our relationships to all the type rays.

Although the concept of a possible next life, and speculation as to what type we will be in the next life, is exciting and fascinating, it is best to forget about the 'next life' because things are determined by forces about which we know nothing. Therefore all our thoughts on the matter are worthless and unable to give us real help. The most important task, right now in this life, is to become a *better version* of our essence type. Fundamental to the 12-type Enneagram purpose is for us to know the expected advantages and flaws of this 'home' type. This is a different perspective for looking at the concepts of 'type limitations' and 'type blindness'.

The purpose of 'moving round' the type path in the correct type order is, on the smaller scale, to *acquire versatility*: to grow and understand about ways of thinking, feeling and acting. *Few people do this.*

It is crucial for the types on the 'personal' or 'younger' side (Lunar, Venus, Mercury types) to learn to be able to think, feel and act with the good characteristics of the 'non-personal' or 'older' side (Saturn, Mars, Jupiter types) – *and vice versa.* For the younger side, consciously accessing the older energies gives the younger types the same advantages that older types are already using (we all compete in the same world – we need the same advantages); for older types, being consciously aware when they are manifesting younger type-energies prevents their being exploited by the consequences of the younger types' inappropriate, immature or irresponsible energy (the managing director who finds it funny to send sexist photos to female staff). And, of course there are many positive advantages for the non-personal types in learning how to access the personal types' essence energies.

Lunar-type Movement through the Enneagram

Since most of the essence energies default to Lunar type, and since we were all once children, there is worth for all of us in studying the Lunar-type movement through the number sequence.

After exposure to the 12-type Enneagram the Lunar-type individual first understands their home-type characteristics, and then moves in a conscious direction round the Enneagram cycle, gathering the other elements needed for a balanced life.

The Lunar-type 'baby' characteristics (total self-centredness, preoccupation with what they need, using 'others' in their world to serve their needs, fixation on their experience as being definitive) have to go through a phase of development where they begin to respect the needs of the others that surround them. The 'baby' type-energy learns, we hope, that screaming is not always the best way to get what it wants. The Lunar type learns some of the ways of the Venus type, and acquires a healthy, attractive interest in caring about others, and thereby gets what they want through more 'grown up' ways of behaviour.

Then they can go through a Mercury-type phase where they become fascinated with the outside world, until the outside world is more interesting to them than the Lunar-type self-centred world. Then they realize the value of focusing on a specific interest (Saturn type) and promoting what they are doing (Mars type). Finally they learn to celebrate and value achievement in Jupiter-type energy.

Baby/Child Development

The description above is close to the natural development process that every baby/child goes through. At the beginning the baby will be interested in nothing but its own needs (Lunar type), then it learns a certain joy from relating to others (Venus-type influence), then it becomes interested in the outer world completely and learns to walk (Mercury-type influence); at first it walks to satisfy its own needs, but then it seeks to 'explore' – not just everything around it, but things/people of *selected* interest about which it feels a need to acquire information (Saturn-type influence). In one of the trips around the 12-type Enneagram, at a certain level, the child goes to school – and learns in an organized way. Coming into contact with peers it feels a need to defend itself (Mars-type influence) and finally begins to learn about loving interactions with others that can lead to an 'everybody wins' situation (Jupiter-type influence).

Throughout this book, what is sought is a balance between conveying knowledge that has, hitherto, been lost to the general world, in a way that respects and contains the essence of its deep meaning and information for us, and providing everyday examples and anecdotes which make the knowledge come alive. While we are reading, inner processes are taking place. Our instinctive centre is absorbing these images and we may suddenly be surprised how, without our consciously working on it, some or other aspect of the knowledge seems lodged inside our understanding. This is part of the joy of having unconscious and hidden resources – resources that come more to the front of our lives as our knowledge of the 12-type Enneagram broadens and deepens.

Chapter 12

Famous Types and Other Topics

Although the system has nothing to say about the craze for celebrity, it is useful to refer to certain well-known people who exemplify a particular essence type. Many of the examples are known to us through films, and have often played characters *who match their essence type.* All the type-examples are no longer with us: it would not be appropriate to name a living person as a particular type.

> **Lunar type:** *Audrey Hepburn.* In films such as *Sabrina, Breakfast at Tiffany's* and *Wait Until Dark,* Audrey is eternally childlike, charming and innocent.
>
> **Lunar–Venus type:** *Marilyn Monroe.* Tragic Marilyn is the archetypal affectionate sexy childlike adult. We love her for her tender vulnerability and innocent beauty. Most of her films reflect these qualities: *Some Like it Hot, Gentlemen Prefer Blondes, Bus Stop, The Misfits.*
>
> **Venus type:** *Elizabeth Taylor.* Elizabeth was always a sexual, sensual woman. She sized up people in physical terms and was not ashamed to 'live for love'. In the last phase of her life she became a committed AIDS campaigner, illustrating Venus type's manifestation of Jupiter type. *Butterfield 8, Cleopatra, Zee & Co.*
>
> **Venus–Mercury type:** *John F Kennedy.* The busy, fun-loving lover hybrid type put sex into the White House. He was the king of Camelot, a magical, make-believe kingdom, apparently removed from the realities of the Vietnam War.
>
> **Mercury type:** *Danny Kaye.* To understand pure Mercury-type energy as opposed to frantic and unfocused freneticism, view Kaye's marvellous, physical co-ordination as he rattles off lyrics while dancing. *Hans Christian Andersen.*

Mercury–Saturn type: Noël Coward. Sophisticated, witty, slick, his life was emblematic of his hybrid type. Highly polished with a high degree of output. *Design for Living, Blithe Spirit.*

Saturn Type: *Sigmund Freud.* The father of psychoanalysis exemplifies the deep-thinking, questioning and philosophical Saturn-type mind.

Saturn–Mars type: *Winston Churchill, Adolf Hitler.* Two examples to illustrate that the same hybrid energy has good and bad representatives.

Mars type: *Clark Gable.* A 'man's man', his warrior–athlete characteristics took him hunting and fishing, camping in primitive conditions far from his sophisticated Hollywood stardom. *Gone With the Wind, It Happened One Night, The Misfits.*

Mars–Jupiter: *Mahatma Gandhi.* There are other wonderful examples of this humanitarian type, Gandhi is chosen because there is newsreel footage in which he illustrates that a person of slight build and gentle manner can still exhibit extraordinary power, strength, determination and idealism.

Jupiter type: *Ingrid Bergman.* Lovely Ingrid, both facially and in terms of her personality. View her Best Supporting Actress speech for an example of this type's selfless generosity. *Casablanca, The Inn of the Sixth Happiness.*

Jupiter–Lunar type: *Maria von Trapp.* Not the real-life woman, but the character as portrayed by Julie Andrews in *The Sound of Music.* She does not have to adapt to the children because she is one. Yet she is also able to take charge and be indignant on their behalf, because she can feel what their father's neglect must mean to them. And although she marries the baron, there is no sexual chemistry (this hybrid needs to go to Venus type to learn about love).

See if you can identify well-known people by observing their words and behaviour. Be aware, though, that nowadays there are few examples of 'pure' essence types because our fast, multi-tasking life, and the dominance of media frenzy, obliges us to remain for long periods of time out of our essence type.

Living in Different Worlds

We already appreciate that we live in different worlds: one person's experience of life will be different from another's. But prior to an introduction to the 12-type Enneagram, we have not understood how many of those differences can be identified and defined. As we continue to explore the system, we find more and more areas where understanding the essence types clarifies and illuminates our lives and those of others we know.

Concepts and Projects

We can refer to the six main Enneagram essence types in order to ensure that a concept we have will develop in the right manner, and not become mired, either in *resistance* or in the propensity for *wrong or mechanical development*. Mechanical development can be observed, for example, in the game 'Chinese Whispers'. The further from the original statement the game goes, the more the actual statement is lost, as individuals add their own interpretation. Finally the result has nothing to do with what was there originally.

To avoid that happening in a concept we have, or a project on which we intend to work, we can develop and guide it through the six type influences. *This sequence holds for all of the types*: the best method is to go through the different type-energies in the order in which they appear in the 'magic numbers' – 1, 4, 2, 8, 5, 7:

1. Lunar-type energy: intuitive thinking, creativity and enthusiasm. This is where we get our concept.
4. Venus type: next we go here to gather *emotional* energy for the task. Most projects have a lengthy time sequence so here we 'fall in love' with our task.
2. Mercury type: thirdly, we progress to this energy influence for the process of researching the background of our concept, to check the competition, to 'do our due diligence'.
8. Saturn type: here we *deepen* our concept and really get to grips with our project. We question from all angles. We think through all the possible options and paths it may go through, iron out the glitches and *really understand* the material with which we are working.

5. Mars type: here we put the concept into *action*. In the practical, earthy energy of Mars type, we access boldness and resilience, necessary for overcoming obstacles and establishing our 'ownership'.
7. Jupiter type: here we actualize the full, beneficial, nature of our concept. We integrate it into the wider picture, and make it available for others to profit by.

The same sequence of type-energies is desirable for practical projects, for example, starting a business:

1. Lunar-type energy: We create the concept for a new shopping experience.
4. Venus type energy: rather than immediately firing off in all directions in Mercury-type energy, we visit Venus-type energy to bring a deep emotional commitment, and *a centred lack of frantic pace*, to the project.
2. Mercury-type energy: here we do our research, plan what is needed for the business, identify potential financial investors.
8. Saturn-type energy: here we put together the information we have gathered, in a deeper way. We calculate gains and potential losses, we question and think through each and every aspect of the business.
5. Mars-type energy: here we approach investors. Because we have 'done our homework' they are impressed with the thoroughness and competence modelled in our presentation. The business goes ahead.
7. Jupiter type energy: here we are rewarded for our work. We see the benefits to others and we take time to value ourselves for a job well done.

It is *always* useful and informative, even when we are already engaged in an endeavour, to consider the information available in the 12-type Enneagram. A situation where we have had an idea, done lightning research, mortgaged our house and have fingers crossed for direct intervention on our behalf from the Lord is not as promising as one in which we have followed the progress of the type-energies in their correct order to minimize our downside and maximize our potential. Therefore, if you are already engaged in a project, consider whether you have engaged with all the type-energies in the correct sequence. If not, you now have the guidelines for introducing and integrating what may be missing into the existing structure.

Animals and the Types

Pet owners will not find it a surprise to read that the 12-type Enneagram influences are also to be discerned in our feline, canine or other loved ones. If you have ever had a pet, you will already know that animals, at least to their owners who see them at their best, have unique personalities. These personalities are reflected in the Enneagram types.

Here are examples of each main Enneagram type, styled for cats:

Lunar type cat: Isolated, a loner but sometimes becomes emotionally needy and demonstrative. Occasionally gets 'scatty' and runs around after nothing. 'Plays' with its own body, twisting itself into shapes that appear to amuse the cat. Sometimes needs a great deal of affection; when it feels secure, it again becomes independent.

Venus-type cat: Loving, extraordinary warmth and real pleasure in greeting us on our return. Sensuous, always seeking lap warmth even on a warm day. Sadly, this type finds change extremely stressful and frightening so take particular care with them when moving home.

Mercury-type cat: Always on the prowl. Summer times are spent with days sleeping in exhaustion, the warm nights circulating around neighbours' gardens. Restless even when sitting in our laps.

Saturn-type cat: Fascinated by water and other unexpected things that pique his or her intellectual interest. Stares out the window at passing cars and pedestrians. Finds unusual items to have fun with, like paper clips or rubber bands.

Mars-type cat: Needs to be in control. Highly choosy over food, will go on hunger strike rather than compromise. Curiously vulnerable in that the cat has to keep re-establishing his/her omnipotence: when we change our sofa position, cat cannot just sit on our laps, he/she has to 'create an incident', jump off, look annoyed and flick tail before possibly returning.

Jupiter-type cat: Determined to make friends among the other cats in the block. Sits patiently for hours while other cats finish territorial howling, then settles down near them. Slow-moving, loving and tolerant.

Like ourselves cats and other animals contain all the energies. Therefore all aspects of behaviour listed may apply to your animal. Nevertheless some behaviours will predominate, leading to type identification.

Using Music to Access Different Type-Energies

It is widely understood that music has great value as an emotional communicator. Although songs will not have been written expressly to manifest the various type-energies, this does not preclude certain songs from embodying the different type-energy qualities. The list should be regarded as a general impression and as a further way of understanding the different type-energies, rather than type 'anthems'. If some songs are unfamiliar they can be heard on the Internet.

> **Lunar type:** Red Rubber Ball; Red, Red Wine; Happy Jack
> **Lunar–Venus type:** I Want to be Loved by You; Running Wild
> **Venus type:** You're My World; Love This is My Song; The First Time Ever I Saw Your Face; 24 Hours from Tulsa
> **Venus–Mercury type:** Get Happy; Sit Right Down and Write Myself a Letter
> **Mercury Type:** I Get Around; It's All for the Best (from *Godspell*)
> **Mercury–Saturn type:** Mad Dogs and Englishmen; Always Look on the Bright Side of Life
> **Saturn Type:** Maybe You're Right; How to Handle a Woman (from *Camelot*)
> **Saturn–Mars Type:** Come Together; Everybody Get Together
> **Mars Type:** We Are the Champions; Love is a Battlefield
> **Mars–Jupiter Type:** Bless the Beasts and Children; Star Spangled Banner; Sing (a Song)
> **Jupiter Type:** Bridge Over Troubled Water; We Have All the Time in the World; Climb Every Mountain; Make Our Garden Grow (from *Candide*)
> **Jupiter–Lunar Type:** Something Good (from *The Sound of Music*); You and Me (from *Victor/Victoria*)

When you listen to the different songs, take note of the mood they bring out in you. We know to look to sad ballads when we are feeling sorry for ourselves. There is a more valuable application in listening to music, however: we can use it as an opportunity to experience different type-energies.

Defining Our Living in Different Worlds

Although we all inhabit the same sphere, the *particular emphases* and the *areas of neglect* that arise out of the singular, specific type-energies result in the same object or concept having different meanings.

Words

Each of the 12 type-energies has a different understanding of many words of fundamental import like 'love' 'honesty', 'friendship', selfishness', 'trust', and so on. In Chapter 3 there were examples of how the types differ in their understanding of 'seriousness' and 'humour'. By now we have examined the different types from a number of aspects and angles, and we can begin to make educated guesses about how each type will use these important words.

Lunar type: This type creates their own inner world, as much as possible independently of external guides. A word like honesty will be interpreted as having to say everything that's on their mind, rather than judging what is helpful to disclose, and what it may be wiser to remain silent about. Because of the type's kindness and generosity, friendship will include lending items as tokens of commitment. Selfishness relates to the Lunar type's need for independence and safety: they believe in whatever they are doing because they know they are putting their life together, and they trust that other people will understand that their motives are essentially honest and will get out of their way. Trust is something Lunar types appear to give away readily; however, only to a certain point, and then the Lunar type trusts no one except themselves.

Lunar–Venus type: Honesty is admitting their confusion, but they are difficult to help because they brush off the concerns of others. They are always on the lookout for friends who will support their chaotic lives, although they will often break appointments at the last minute if something more 'sexy' appears. Selfishness is done innocently. Trust is given readily, sometimes to complete strangers, because of the type's curious lack of concern about danger or their fondness for playing around with potentially hazardous scenarios.

Venus type: Honesty here is emotional, and Venus types have an extraordinary ability to justify to themselves (and others if they let them) their intense and complex personal relationships: 'I'm always true to you, Darling – in my fashion.' Friendships are their particular talent and they will endure situations that others would walk away from. However, they are extremely sensitive to being disrespected. They dislike open confrontation and may, if they discover gossip about themselves, internalize a psychic wound. Selfishness is not something they agonize over, rather it is understood as a necessary underpinning from which they can display themselves for the enhancement of others' lives. The lover is trusted, and the Venus type makes extravagant declarations to bind the lover to them. 'Hell hath no fury' applies to both female and male Venus types in sexual jealousy.

Venus–Mercury type: Honesty is a complicated scenario of putting themselves down, while at the same time seeking compliments on their physical appearance. Friendships are well maintained, although this type will change friendship circles over time since they know not all friendships are for ever. Selfishness is subtle: things have to be their way or they immediately become silent and absent. Trust is given but over time the type learns to really trust only very, very few.

Mercury type: Honesty for this type is openness. Because of their speed, tact and subtlety eludes them. Selfishness is more to do with their having so many interests rather than type negativity. Trust is expected as a matter of course; the type does not examine situations deeply and does not consider whether or not to 'trust' unless they have been deeply hurt.

Mercury–Saturn type: Honesty is sharing their accomplishments and stresses, which is done readily. Friendships are important, but they may disappear for periods while they are up to some project or other. Selfishness is often surprising: the other side did not understand the secretive nature of this type, seemingly open but under the surface exploring the deeper Saturn-type world. They may experience themselves as open and trustworthy while others find them difficult to read.

Saturn type: Honesty may be an acknowledgment of what they have not accomplished or understood; otherwise the Saturn type keeps their self-doubts to themselves. Friendships involve teaching, sharing knowledge, or items of mutual interest. Selfishness is built into the need for long periods of isolation for reflection. Trust is slower to be given and usually only in the light of observing how the other has behaved. Belief in the other is important for the Saturn type; they need projects of value and don't like to waste time and energy.

Saturn–Mars type: Honesty is revealing the sides of themselves they wish to share. Selfishness is a given, since the type's focus on levering themselves into key positions means ruthlessness. Friendship involves being a part of their working plan, otherwise they do not have friends just for the sake of someone's parties to attend. Trust is more about trusting *them*.

Mars type: Honesty is relative: people are told what they need to hear. Friendship is strong, productive and explicitly or implicitly controlling. Whether or not the Mars type's agenda is visible, and whether or not they began with one, at some point the Mars type's agenda will be revealed; at this point they will confess with a smile, which will fade abruptly if they are contradicted. Selfishness comes from the type's lack of interest in 'smaller' emotions: they believe that in order for them to succeed they *have* to climb over others, and subordinate them. To the Mars type, selfishness is only practical. They may trust family members who have proven themselves time after time but the type's combustible energy is always burning, always alive for signs that others are not trustworthy.

Mars–Jupiter type: Honesty is simplicity in their own lives, a scrupulous examination of what they can do without. Friendship is generous although this type devotes most of their energy to their greater causes. Selfishness is never for the self, but for the greater good, and they expect the other side to understand this. Trust in others is readily offered, although they always take into account people's foibles and inadequacies so they are not too disappointed when the other side lacks their ideals and energy.

Jupiter type: Honesty and humour are intertwined: they laugh at the follies of others and themselves. Friendship is open-armed, warm and generous. They have difficulty with expressing selfishness and will apologize effusively if they need anything for themselves. Trust is implicit in their generosity although they do learn that some people need to be forgiven and avoided rather than blindly trusted.

Jupiter–Lunar type: Honesty is paramount, but sometimes with too much information since the child side hasn't learned to précis. Friendships are very important and this type's social circle will include friends from school all the way up to friends from their current work. Selfishness is complicated since the type is generous to others, but every now and then they realize they have to do something for themselves, and may even 'disappear', a change of approach which confuses the other side. Trust is given readily; when they are let down they are sincerely wounded, but trust will again be offered in the next situation.

Type Differences in Getting Stuck

Each type has their different version of 'getting stuck'. We on the outside may be able to help because we are not caught up in their particular type blindness/limitations. However, we may miss the meaning of what is happening, because we are not relating the *situation* to the *type*. When we do, we may discover that the apparent problem is based more on the type-energy than on a real/serious situation. For this reason, the more we approach the other with the knowledge of their type, the more we will know what – if anything – we should do.

Lunar type: Often get stuck in an obsessive way of thinking. Other types take this so seriously they fail to notice when the Lunar type has totally forgotten the original idea or thought – like children who wildly proclaim that 'X' is no longer their friend because . . . And the parent, worrying about the issue and taking it seriously, fails to notice that the children are playing together again.

Venus type: Stuck with the idea that if they have a relationship, life will be 'perfect'. When they do find a relationship, and life is not perfect, they may have to break up in order to look for the 'perfect relationship' somewhere else. We have to take the shifting emotional sands seriously because they believe that the love relationship is the most important thing in life.

Mercury type: Get stuck in being up with the latest trends. They have many interests and these are ambitious, involving the participation of others, who may not share the Mercury type's enthusiasm or energy and thus projects go on 'hold'.

Saturn type: Get stuck in being profound. Reject any lightness or inconsequentiality and feel guilty when they fool around. 'Deadly seriousness' is appropriate when applied to important issues but can be draining for others if black is the only colour the Saturn type wears, and everything, however light, is given the same heavy intellectual treatment.

Mars type: The slightly deranged Mars type will get stuck in having to be right and in control in matters. Not being able to admit to a mistake becomes a barrier to progression. The healthy Mars type may get stuck in athleticism as a way of life and have to endure many sports injuries.

Jupiter type: Get stuck in carer role. Feel guilty when they are not constantly thinking of others. Healthy Jupiter types recognize the necessity for downtime and personal enjoyment. Can get stuck in having to prove their worth, over and over, through self-sacrifice.

So once you understand the *type* of issue or problem an individual faces, we can apply the correct *balance* to enable the person to access a solution outside their type blindness/limitation. In a following chapter we will enlarge on the theme of negative emotions as they pertain to the different types.

Different Speeds of Behaviour

We have already learned that the six different type-energies operate at different speeds. Now we will consider how this affects their relations with themselves and other types.

- No other type understands why Jupiter type takes so long to 'get going'. The reason is that Jupiter types are feeling more deeply and often have many inner conflicts and different thoughts to consider first, that less deep types do not.

- Undeveloped Lunar types think extremely superficially because they have already made up their minds. Important issues may be decided on a whim or a piece of irrelevant information that crosses their path at the crucial moment. They may pride themselves on 'always knowing the answer' but it will be the first that seems 'right' and they may have plucked it out of the air.
- Mercury and Mars types believe the most important thing is to do *something*. Mercury type will focus on organization; Mars will seek to gain control. Both take little time to think through the likely outcome and even though both types think rapidly, the results reflect this.
- Saturn, Mars–Jupiter, Jupiter and Jupiter–Lunar types move, think and feel more slowly because they do everything more deeply. Mars types can *think* or *do* but only one of the two at a time.
- Venus types may spend most of the time lounging around and avoiding effort, then accomplish whatever they need to do surprisingly quickly. In this way they deal with the issue in Mercury type, then with a sigh resume the Venus type's preferred rhythm.

Different Concepts of Taste

'One man's meat is another man's poison.' The adage could be interpreted as acknowledging that it is *type differences* that are responsible for differences in taste.

- The universally acceptable good taste in clothing that Venus types espouse will not at all be in sync with the usually unique, quirky, taste of Lunar types.
- Mercury types will not understand why their Saturn-type friends didn't enjoy an evening of light comedy. Saturn types, for an evening's entertainment, will suggest watching Bergman's *The Seventh Seal* or *The Sorrow and the Pity*.

- Venus types will sit through soap opera personal dramas that mean nothing to other types. Mars types like blood sports; Jupiter types shudder.
- Lunar types decorate in bright, primary colours; red, yellow, blue. Venus types prefer subtle shades, soft yellows, rich autumn hues, emerald green. Mercury types have beds piled high with papers they never get round to filing. Saturn types don't concern themselves with décor. Mars types admire black leather and steel. Jupiter types may have given away their most admired items. What is left will incorporate the full colour spectrum.
- Mercury types watch motor racing and water skiing, while Venus types watch the ballet. Mars types like competitive sports. Jupiter types cut the oranges for half time.
- Venus–Mercury types seek out emotional musicals and feel-good comedies; Mercury–Saturn types seek out snappy and sophisticated stories; Mars types watch simplistic good/bad stories where the aggressive hero triumphs. Venus types enjoy a good romance, particularly when love brings financial stability. Mars types prefer scenarios in which the lover knows his/her place. Jupiter types love stories of personal redemption and the triumph of the human will over dreadful adversity.
- Mercury–Saturn types are interested in educational and cultural events; Saturn–Mars and Mars–Jupiter types have no interest in things that don't have 'worth', although they will get involved in a fundraising activity if it furthers their social/political agenda. With Saturn–Mars types the event will also promote *them*: Mars–Jupiter types prefer to work and then dodge the applause.
- Lunar–Venus types invest in sensuous clothes that get them into sexual trouble. Mars types may invest in shaky financial schemes or, worse, be guarantor for someone else's scheme, because *they are over-confident that things will work.* They never admit to self-doubt even if they know an enterprise is a risk. Mars businessmen have boom–bust careers because the crude energy of the type seems to indicate little alternative (they don't like 'little' emotions, so they don't get involved in 'little' projects that may be safer).

Physical Exercise, Sport and the Types

For many children, love of, or antipathy to, sport and physical exercise can be the difference between a happy or a troubled childhood and adolescence. For example, Lunar types may become overwhelmed by trauma, even just the trauma of being alive, and seek solace in overeating, thus making sports an ongoing nightmare. Saturn types will pursue academic achievement to offset their failure in sports. Although individual circumstances can affect someone's interest in, or anathema towards, sport and physical exercise, generally the types tend to evince enthusiasm or otherwise according to observable type distinctions:

> **Lunar type:** Most popular are games that involve 'play' – rounders, baseball, football, wrestling. The Lunar type may or may not take sports seriously, depending on whether they stay within their Lunar self-world: they can also default into Mars-type energy and become fiercely competitive. Engaging in exercise can be particularly beneficial for Lunar types, since it may give them time off from their constant inner dialogue.
>
> **Venus type:** Observing people working out at a gym, we note how the best-dressed examples tend to do three sets of a single-effort action, then stop for a while, during which they will check themselves out in a mirror or talk to friends. The slower energy rate of 72 beats a minute means that they will probably spend longer in the gym than will a Mercury or Mars type to accomplish the same level of work-out. Venus types enjoy water sports as well as dancing, acrobatics, and anything that brings together the physical body and physical grace. Their love of the physical can lead to making their whole life about exercise and sport, becoming personal trainers or professional athletes.
>
> **Mercury type:** Long-distance running, triathlon, tennis, badminton, squash, rowing – games with a lengthy personal commitment, and physical dexterity/fluidity. This type-energy most exemplifies the *moving centre* and they will prefer bicycles for getting around.
>
> **Saturn type:** Notable for their antipathy towards sports generally, Saturn types may become horse-racing

commentators, or other sports pundits. If their health demands a degree of exercise this will tend to be the gentle varieties: walking, swimming, bowls. They may be chess players or favour other games of skill.

Mars type: As already noted, Mars type's love of competition finds a natural home in sports. Boxing, wrestling, weightlifting, ju-jitsu and other martial arts are popular. Physical exercise is viewed as a personal challenge, so a Mars type may decide to sort out a bog garden in mid-winter (to challenge nature's cold, wet, smelly extremes). Pilates is also appealing since it builds core strength – they like their muscles to feel 'like steel'.

Jupiter type: Jupiter types are content to sit on the sidelines and shout friendly encouragement to the players. Where they do get interested in physical activity it will be prompted by the spiritual/philosophic aspect of the activity, such as in the various schools of yoga. They will also follow the gentler forms of exercise and may indulge themselves in what is almost an exercise: having a massage.

Holidays

Lunar type: Like a certain amount of exploration, but not too much (imagine children on planes, crying because they're over-tired).

Lunar–Venus type: Look for destinations where they can explore themselves sexually.

Venus type: Look for sunshine, lying on a beach or, alternatively, ski holidays where they can wear the trendiest outfits.

Venus–Mercury type: Destinations with lots of nightlife.

Mercury type: Multi-destination, the 'If it's Tuesday, this must be Belgium' approach.

Mercury–Saturn type: Sophisticated destinations they can drop into conversations.

Saturn type: Worthwhile visits. Prior to departure, much research on what needs to be seen.

Saturn–Mars type: Destinations where *they* can shine.

Mars type: Only have to go to the same place more than once and they believe they 'own' it.

Mars–Jupiter type: Destinations are part of their busy political/social agenda.

Jupiter type: Developing countries where they seek out projects and make a difference.

Jupiter–Lunar type: Visiting friends and places they've always wanted to see.

Chapter 13

Accessing the Type-Energy Two Types Ahead

As we move – or bounce – our way *unconsciously* round the 12-type Enneagram, we will at times be two types ahead of our own essence type. This chapter is concerned with exploring the very great and real benefits of *consciously* accessing the type-energy two types ahead of us:

Home type	*Two types ahead*
Lunar/Lunar–Venus types	Mercury type
Venus/Venus–Mercury types	Saturn type
Mercury/Mercury–Saturn type	Mars type
Saturn/Saturn–Mars type	Jupiter type
Mars/Mars–Jupiter type	Lunar type
Jupiter/Jupiter–Lunar type	Venus type

Already, just by reading the list, we start to see the beneficial possibilities of such a conscious effort.

Lunar Type

We imagine someone enthusiastic, childlike, kindly in their approach; someone always ready to drop work and play at something or other. Someone who spends time each day dreaming in their SelfWorld. Someone who has difficulty trusting, or taking advice unless they have decided it is worthwhile. Someone who likes their independence but is always looking to make connections with others; a surprisingly loyal and often generous friend.

The Lunar type will create a set of facts about the world, and then live their lives as though their inventions are objectively true. They may be up to all sorts of interesting things, but they may not believe they can ever make something of themselves, which is why they turn to their SelfWorld for comfort, security and balance. It is helpful for Lunar type consciously to access Mercury-type energy because the Lunar-type world is obsessively inner-self. By consciously accessing Mercury-type energy they get outside themselves and they get organized.

However, the desirability of this access through *conscious effort* is stressed, rather than Lunar type accidentally or through unconscious default accessing the Mercury-type energy: Lunar type first needs to go to Venus type to acquire some self-care because the foundation of slower, 72 beats a minute Venus-type energy will be helpful once they are in the fast-paced Mercury-type 144 beats a minute. If Mercury type is accessed without Venus type self-care, the Lunar type will become lost in frantic activity and tire themselves out.

The Lunar–Venus types are more aware of the physical dimension, since they are influenced by earth-bound Venus-type energy. However, they still benefit from consciously accessing Mercury-type energy because they tend to slow down and get lost in fantasy/feelings, and have even more problems than the Lunar type in getting the elements of their lives together. Generally, while in Mercury type, Lunar/Lunar–Venus type can accomplish all the *Outer*world tasks they've been unable to complete because Lunar-type energy has difficulty with *process*. The ability to process from start to conclusion is accessed through the Mercury-type energy.

Venus Type

We have come to know Venus type as languid, slow-moving, sensuous individuals, centred on clothes and personal appearance and in talking for hours about emotional issues, or watching fairly interchangeable TV soap operas which are distinguished only by the *frantic drama* and *intense anxiety* in which the characters 'live'. Venus type live in their *emotional* sense for their contact with the world. Remember, though, they *admire* intelligence and may seek to marry it. Therefore it is highly advantageous for Venus type consciously to go two types ahead and access Saturn-type energy for themselves.

It is preferable that the Venus type consciously advances through Mercury type. Speeding up takes the Venus type out of their characteristic languor; it reminds them that they have other abilities. Once in Mercury-type energy, the Venus type turns towards Saturn type. Here the Venus type crosses The Divide that exists between the 'younger' and 'older' types.

As was noted earlier in the case of the person who thought they were a Venus–Saturn type split, if someone is going to give up the Venus-type *insight* temporarily, they need to be sure that they are accessing Saturn-type depth of thought, not that they are imagining it (which would be them defaulting to unprofitable Lunar-type fantasy). Venus types, and particularly Venus–Mercury hybrid types, *can* think intellectually, although this tends to be only on specific projects or subjects. They can develop this by getting into the habit of asking 'Why?' of their lives.

Mercury Type

We think of Mercury type as our well-organized individuals. They can be relied on for factual information and we turn to them when we have deliveries to be made, or organizational deadlines to be met. We remember that Mercury is the last of the three 'younger' types, and that the path of inner spiritual and psychological progress is to cross The Divide and access the deep Saturn-type energy. This also gives us an inkling as to why it is helpful and valuable for Mercury type consciously to access two types ahead: Mars type.

Mercury types often find themselves in administrative and lower-middle-management positions. Some are happy here but some would prefer more management responsibilities. They may have observed of themselves that if they use just speed, or if they micro-manage their staff and don't let them get on with their jobs, they end up with a feeling of disappointment, a sense that they haven't been up to the task. By consciously accessing first Saturn-type energy to think about the situation, and then Mars energy, Mercury types acquire the most important element of what their type-energy is missing: earth-grounded control and managing ability.

Because they have often been around the seat of power embodied by Mars-type energy, Mercury types can make a success of this conscious jump two-types-forward. For example, the personal assistant to a member of parliament, in her 'spare time', is the chairperson of a local charity. By Mercury type consciously accessing Mars type, she can put into practice for herself the experience of wielding power, and with the type's customary speed she is often the only one who reads all the documents on the board's agendas. The essential point for Mercury type, in consciously accessing Mars type, is that it helps them to experience a more rounded and complete sense of their life. By not confining themselves to 'support' roles, the Mercury type may become more at peace, less bothered by the type's inner dissatisfaction that keeps them perpetually on the lookout for new directions.

Saturn Type

The serious, questioning, profound nature of the Saturn type will naturally turn his or her attention to the greater question: the state of humankind. Therefore it might seem that for Saturn type to access the energy influence two types ahead, Jupiter type, is an easy matter. It is true that the relative distance between the two on the 12-type Enneagram is not far, and it is also true that since the Saturn type loves sharing or imparting knowledge, a Jupiter-type influence is never far from their natural operating style. However, it is always useful for Saturn types *consciously* to access Jupiter-type energy. For example, a Saturn type may become excited about the intellectual problem of solving some issue, which for the people concerned is a matter of life or death: by consciously accessing Jupiter type, the Saturn type accesses the human elements and realizes that it is these that are of paramount importance.

As with all the types, moving to the influence of Jupiter type is always valuable because it takes each individual type out of their type-blindness, which is operationally and objectively a limitation, and opens up the bigger picture (however, it obviously does not take Jupiter type out of its own type-blindness). An undeveloped Saturn type may become so fixed on proving some tiny point, valuable only to themselves, that they are not factoring in the time/effort element; although they prize worth, they are caught up in a process without value (they have defaulted to a slightly deranged Lunar type pseudo-energy). By consciously accessing Jupiter-type energy they ensure their ability to consider issues deeply is not sidetracked or cheapened by the Lunar-type default.

Mars Type

Mars-type energy embodies an exciting sense of physicality and movement, of bold challenges and resilience. The fiery energy of Mars type, unless balanced by moving towards Jupiter type, can become derailed and slightly 'deranged' so that they cannot take feedback and have to be in charge, down to dictating when they will meet and what will be talked about (only topics safe for the Mars type, not ' personal feedback'). They may lose friendships because friends become overly controlled and dominated.

To explain to a Mars type that it would be helpful to move two types forward *consciously* to Lunar type may be met with irritation or worse. In any case, they would say, they *default* to Lunar type so, to them, what would be the point? The point is that when Mars type defaults to Lunar type they don't take on the authentic childlike innocence of Lunar type. What they do is a Mars type *imitation*: they may believe they are in Lunar type, but the limitation is often clumsy and crude. Again, it is necessary to move first to Jupiter-type energy in order to let go of the tightly bound control and embrace the selfless love embodied by Jupiter type.

If a Mars type *truly* accesses the energy of Lunar type, through conscious effort, he or she will see the difference. Rather than the dominating play they have previously experienced, they will discover how Lunar type's profound lack of guile and perennial innocence creates a world the Mars type could access, if they learn to let go of the 'champion' aspect of the type energy, and discover the fun of not caring and not being serious that the Lunar type enjoys. As well as the benefits to their own health, if a Mars type can consciously access Lunar-type energy it will show others their more vulnerable side, and this will have benefits in terms of their friendship circle. Also, Lunar type is always interested in *learning*, whereas Mars-type energy is dismissive of it, so by going to this type Mars type can grow in areas they miss in their own essence type. They can learn to celebrate the humility of *not* being right. Mars types sometimes need to be challenged by others. When they have it proved to them that they are incorrect in some way, perhaps not following the rules of the gym, Mars type will take the 'correction' silently and grimly. By consciously accessing Lunar type they can give a light shrug, an 'OK', and dismiss the lessen as learned.

Jupiter Type

The warm, readily laughing, instinctively caring Jupiter type is attractive to other types. However, the prospective friend or lover may become disheartened because the base of the Jupiter impulse is not one-to-one intensity or lust: it's a selfless love for, and interest in, humanity. By consciously accessing the two-types-ahead energy influence of Venus type, the Jupiter type moves beyond their 'selfless love', and begins to explore their one-to-one emotional and sexual needs. Before accessing Venus-type energy, it is beneficial for Jupiter type to go through Lunar-type energy. This is helpful specifically because of Jupiter type's 'selflessness'. In Lunar type, self-obsessed and seeing the world entirely through themselves, Jupiter type picks up the idea and the experience of having a constantly inward-looking SelfWorld. Where there was a selfless *vacuum*, in Lunar type the Jupiter type acquires an understanding of *why* it is important to self-consider. They also enjoy some of the isolation and independence in the form of 'not caring' that Lunar-type energy embodies.

Then they can move down to the self-involved emotional world of the Venus type. Some Jupiter types may wonder why this is helpful; why can't they just continue to put out radiant energy, encouraging and supporting whomever they encounter? For some Jupiter types, particularly those who are the Jupiter–Lunar hybrid type, there is a perennial puzzle as to why their relationships become 'sexless' and fizzle out. Like all people, Jupiter types do have personal needs: by consciously accessing Venus-type energy, the Jupiter type acquires sufficient one-to-one emotional skills to understand how to operate on an intimate basis.

The Jupiter–Lunar hybrid type, during moments when they are more influenced by Lunar-type energy, will be more focused on the idea of finding a supportive partner. While in Jupiter-type energy they will not see further than being on their own at someone's wedding, and being sincerely pleased for the happy couple. But the influence of the lonely Lunar type will cause a poignant desire in them to also have a significant other. This then helps the hybrid type to be more enthusiastic about consciously accessing Venus-type energy, in order to learn the secrets of maintaining the one-to-one relationship.

For this type consciously to access Venus-type energy is particularly important if they long for a family. This brings us to our next subject: in the next chapter we will consider children in the light of the 12-type Enneagram.

Chapter 14

Looking at Children Through the Enneagram

Handle with Care

Author's Note: While I was bringing together the material for this chapter I was surprised to find my thoughts seemingly irrelevantly occupied by the image of a gun in the act of being loaded. Having dismissed the image, only to have it spontaneously return, I pondered on it and realized this is precisely the potential 'blowback' involved in writing about observing children through the prism of the wisdom of the 12-type Enneagram. Handled with respect and used carefully, a gun may protect. Mishandling may lead to loss of control and accidents. Therefore, when considering our children, and the whole subject of children, in the light of the types, we must be even more cautious than normal.

There are several reasons for this, but the principal one is that *we may not be right.* We may not have enough information, or we may be misinterpreting the information, and a wrong decision could have severe consequences. For example, let us say a particular boy expresses an interest in understanding the human body. His delighted parents decide from this one example that he is either a Saturn, Saturn–Mars, Mars, Mars–Jupiter or Jupiter type and deluge him with technical books and other educational material. As it transpires, his transitory interest in the human body rapidly wanes and the parents watch as he transfers this early passion onto a more lasting interest: cricket. He becomes a professional cricketer, which fits well with his actual essence type, which is Lunar type. Children generally may take many, many directions before finding one that fits. Cautious interest is better than over-enthusiasm followed by a disappointed parental 'You always do this.'

Obviously a misdiagnosis of type is not the only reason for a child to be pushed in one direction rather than another. Children are forced to go to the same school as their father, or to be interested in the same activities as their mother, and this has taken place entirely without a wrongly applied 'knowledge' of the 12-type Enneagram. However, since this knowledge is now being offered openly to the reading public, it is vital that we do not begin with any initial misunderstandings. So to repeat, the aim is information: in this context it is a 'this-is-what-there-is' rather than a 'how-to' book. So when we look at a child and wonder which type he or she may grow into, it is only to have more information, *never to try to 'fix' or change the child* the better to 'fit' them into one type rather than another.

Again, the reason for this is that *our judgment may be wrong.* As the years progress, the child will most probably lose some of the 'characteristics' on which we might base an incorrect 'diagnosis'.

Another example here is of a girl who expresses an interest in becoming a ballet dancer. Her mother assumes her to be a Venus type, and believes her daughter capable of the complicated Venus-type/Mars-type *resilience* needed to cope with the physical demands. Although she has the look, and is fairly graceful, her daughter struggles among girls more naturally type-suited to the ballet. The mother determinedly drags her daughter to lessons while the child becomes more and more unhappy. Eventually the daughter is so distraught that the mother is forced to remove her. The daughter takes to her bedroom, discovers the world of knowledge, and in early adulthood turns her early interest in ballet into a career researching and lecturing on the history of theatrical costume: she is a Saturn type.

Therefore, in seeking to understand what types our children may be, we are not doing this in order to influence or change them, or even to put one path of development in their way rather than another, *we are interested only in understanding them better.* Observation may lead us to decide that our children are one type or another, but we should hesitate to use this information to shape or limit.

Reviewing Images from our own Childhood

Before turning our attention to our own children, and in order to acquire the taste for being more *accurate* in our observations, let us explore our own childhoods.

- Can you recall the children who went on to become 'prefects', 'class leaders' or 'head of year': what were the identifying marks of someone who stood out from the rest? Here we would tend to find Saturn, Saturn–Mars, Mars, Mars–Jupiter and Jupiter types.
- Who were the 'cool' kids? What made them such? Probably not academic success, more likely athletic ability or being in trouble with authority. Here we would find Mars types (rebelling against the control of others), Lunar types (making friends laugh) and Venus and Mercury types (latest clothes, hair styles, new words and technology).
- Who were the needy kids? What do you remember about the way they behaved? One example is of a boy who dreamed away the year, and spent the last minutes before exams, while others were frantically cramming information, drawing pictures on his work pad. He was a Lunar type. The others thought him 'weird' and 'funny': he was actually taking refuge from the distress of not knowing how to learn by turning inward to his SelfWorld.
- Who were the quiet kids? Sometimes this means a Saturn type or Jupiter type. Unlikely to be a Mars or Mercury type.
- The Lunar-type kid may appear to be an exhibitionist or show-off; this relates to the idea that 'negative attention is better than no attention'. What this child needs is support for finding themselves.

Were *you* a 'cool kid', a 'leader kid', a 'needy kid' or a 'quiet kid'?

Which type influences do you believe contribute to a happy childhood, and which to an unhappy one? The answer here may be less obvious than it appears: although 'Lunar type' would seem to be the ideal for a real 'child's childhood', if the outside circumstances are not good – if the parents get divorced, if there is friction in the union, no union at all or if they are living in a troubled environment – the Lunar type's sense of *being easily overwhelmed* will swamp the child's natural and instinctive sense of play.

More Examples of Child to Adult Type Development

- The popular 'head boy' gets into severe difficulties after leaving school. Tall and good looking, a Venus type, he had allowed the school world to revolve around him, floating along on other people's expectations, only adequate in exam results. Given his popularity and personal charm, after leaving school much is expected of him: instead he finds a 'little' job in a clothes shop, where he can be surrounded by fashion and does not have to think. His parents never get over his 'failure' and as he progresses into his twenties he suffers with psychological issues.
- A family with three children moves next door to where a four-year-old deaf child is living. Although the two brothers make their way in the world of electronic communication (Mercury and Mercury–Saturn types), the little girl from the age of six virtually adopts the deaf girl as her intimate friend. When the time comes for choosing a career it becomes inevitable that she will elect to work with deaf children (she is a Jupiter type).
- Two sisters find different ways of reacting to the discord in their parents' marriage. The one seeks validation by being involved with 'boys', and has a baby at 17 (Lunar–Venus type); her sister sorrowfully searches out someone she can love in a sacrificial way and puts up with a physically abusive boyfriend (Jupiter type).
- Two brothers: the older by two years is warm and trusting and dotes on his younger brother until the younger one goes to school and breaks away from the close-knit family. Then he bullies his older brother who, after a psychological struggle, comes out as gay and becomes a therapist for gay men (the older is developed Lunar type; the younger undeveloped Mars type).
- Four sisters: the oldest has a share in bringing up the youngest, and chooses a career as a flight attendant

(Venus–Mercury type). The second marries a widower who already has four children (Jupiter type). The third never marries, and devotes herself to her ageing parents (Lunar type). The youngest becomes a catwalk model (Venus type).

- A family of three children. The oldest becomes a doctor at 22 (Mars–Jupiter type); the second son becomes confused and lost in the world of finance (Lunar type); the daughter gives up a promising career as a classical singer to pursue the financial benefits of a career in the City (Mars type).

Nature? Nurture?

In the process of putting together this chapter, I asked my teacher: 'Are we born a type from the womb? is it within our DNA? How soon in the development of a child do you know what type he or she is?'

His answer was:

'We are born with our type already determined. You can see the early signs. Group the information by the three functional group types rather than individual types:

- The **moving** function types (Mercury and Mars) simply 'move' more than the other types. Their hands are busy. They often crawl/walk earlier than other types and often have better movement skills. When they want something, they reach out . . . walk to . . . often cry or make noise (by pounding blocks or hitting things) . . . they often throw their toys.
- The **intellectual** function types (Lunar and Saturn) tend to cry less; young Lunar types sometimes blink a lot, trying to see better; from the moment their eyes can see with some relative precisions, they entertain/amuse themselves by discovering/examining things; they speak earlier and often learn to read earlier.
- The **emotional** function types (Venus and Jupiter) want to be in the company of 'mummy' and other people in general; they are often better-natured than the other types and they 'want' less. They feel a noticeable comfort just 'being in their bodies' that is not present in other types. They are usually graceful.'

The Natural Arising of a Child's Type Tendencies

In seeking to understand and support our child, we are aware that each type will view a situation, issue, or even a noun or verb differently.

The Concept of 'Playing'

Although this is a generational cliché, it is also true that this generation of children is catered to and aimed at by the forces of commercialization more than ever before. The idea that children should ever be bored seems to have become taboo, rather than understanding that this is the way in which children should learn to *tolerate* boredom and frustration. Since many children's idea of 'play' is sitting in front of a TV screen or a computer, or working a hand-held device, traditional differences in how essence types play have become blurred. However, it is still possible for parents or carers to provide a more stimulating and imaginative environment for the child, rather than relying on the electronic advantages that are also disadvantages in encouraging *independent and appropriate* essence-type thought and behaviour in our children.

All children play, so by viewing our children's play in the light of the 12-type Enneagram definitions, it may help us to understand our particular child better:

Lunar: Get involved physically, don't consider their clean clothes. Lose themselves in imagination. Create elaborate stories.

Venus: Staying neat is important. Complicated loyalty/friendship/rivalry patterns. Prefer playing with *one* other.

Mercury: Play involves going places. May have a number of friends for different activities. Natural organizers of team sports. Will leave sports equipment and clothes wherever they go.

Saturn: Try to outwit computer games. Develop esoteric interests to which much attention is given. Given the chance, will explain rules and philosophy/psychology of games to others.

Mars: Athletic, dominate the playground group. Will form gangs and compete with other gang leaders for dominance.

Jupiter: Will be alert for waifs and strays, both other children and animals. Play will involve situations in which the child can care for another (hospital healing scenarios, teacher teaching slower friend to read, mother caring for child, and so on).

Child's WorldView

Different type-energies in the child focus on different aspects of the world. Sometimes these aspects are forced on the child by divorce, multiple locations, deprivation and other factors. If we consider the overall WorldView of the different types as manifested in children, we realize that by understanding how our child views the world we can then *support* them to widen and strengthen their understanding, and better protect them from their fears and doubts.

Lunar: The world is magical, wondrous. The shape of a flower is a delight. Yet life is also terrifying and confusing and the child is easily overwhelmed. This type will benefit the most from having things explained to them. May be terrified by images of violence or horror films.

Venus: The world is full of colour and beauty. Also many pretty things that they can own. Friendships are vitally important and central. Need their perception of the primacy of emotional well-being reinforced

Mercury: The world is movement. Seeing as much of it as possible is a major goal and gives them a sense of personal worth.

Saturn: The world is fascinating. Everything needs to be questioned. Sustained pondering on the big issues and ideas involved in living. They need to have their child-seriousness valued and respected.

Mars: The world owes the child a proper living: 'Since I'm alive, what are *you* going to do to make it worth my while?' The world is a battleground and they are always ready for a fight. Or they will pick the fight themselves.

Jupiter: The world is in great need. Terrible things happen and I am somehow culpable. I must do what I can to make things better for those around me. 'I don't do enough – perhaps I can send my pocket money to Africa?'

If we see how different these WorldViews are, it follows that each different type of child will have different perspectives and goals. By listening and watching we can learn about how each child *differently* makes sense of things. Screening out parts of life does not mean that the child is not somewhere aware of them, only that they either don't want, or cannot bear, to look at these parts. For instance, the children of a family living under a right-wing regime spend as much time as possible reading comics and playing computer games: this is because they cannot deal with the reality of the dictatorship, so they turn to the oblivion of other, fantasy existences, being Lunar types. Other children, in the same circumstances, would turn to sport (Mercury/Mars types) or become involved early on in politics and argument with their peers (Saturn/Saturn–Mars/Mars/Mars–Jupiter types).

Childhood and the Hybrids

In addition to the information on the two individual essence energies, which will be observed in the behaviour of the hybrid-type child, the following pertain:

> **Lunar–Venus type**: Safeguarding this most vulnerable of the types begins in childhood. The 'argument' advanced by an abuser of 'the kid wanted it too' may be nothing else than the child's innocent expression of this type-energy's preoccupation with sexual matters. This explanation is offered as a warning to responsible adults, not as any form of excuse for an abuser. It is an abomination that the child's essence energy is exploited and it is the responsibility of the parent, guardian or other to encourage the child to develop Venus-type *sexual scrupulousness* and *responsible self-care.*
> **Venus–Mercury type**: Although this type is 'busy' and 'fun-loving' this will not always manifest in straightforward 'party time' behaviour. Individuals will find their *own* expression of 'fun-loving', particularly if they emphasise the *emotional* over the *speed*. They may favour marathon or tri-athletic training, turn to the priesthood or spend endless hours poring over computers. All will be the *individual's* expression of their type characteristics.
> **Mercury–Saturn type**: The parent may be concerned that their child is spreading themselves too thinly – activities,

commitments, friendships. This hybrid will not thank you for limiting their activities, but they can still benefit if we remember their tendency for speed over depth – and help them to balance their lives, and to place their effort and sense of worth in more deserving areas.

Saturn–Mars type: This hybrid will be frustrated until they can find an arena big enough to contain and promote them. Peer jealousy may cause them to become unpopular. Encouraging them to quietly go about learning what interests them may help, as does reminding them that childhood is not for ever and the tolerance for frustration they learn in these early years will be an advantage in the adult world.

Mars–Jupiter types: This hybrid may experience great difficulty in childhood and adolescence because they see clearly the inequality and agony of the world, and are frustrated by their peers' lack of interest. This hybrid may early on find ways to elevate themselves into the adult world – volunteering after school and being outstanding generally. However, due to any number of circumstances, it may take this hybrid a long time to discover where they wish to place their *worth*, and in the meantime they may flounder in mediocrity and frustration.

Jupiter–Lunar types: In childhood these hybrids may find their adult/responsible type influence more valued than their Lunar type vulnerability. Early on they will be thrust into 'adult' roles that may leave them yearning for the experience of being looked after rather than being the responsible one. Adult Jupiter–Lunar types, even those with power and influence, may talk in a surprisingly soft, childlike way. In childhood we can observe the fantasy of Lunar type but also the universal concerns. This type of child may grows up with unexpressed, deep-rooted self-judgement and criticism. Be aware that the hybrid's early sense of responsibility can mask their own needs.

Supporting Different Type Manifestations

A family includes a son they once found wearing one of the mother's dresses. The parents seized on this and proceeded to buy the child a dress of his own and encouraged him to wear it round the house. The parents told their friends, who told their children, so the child's secret became a source of ridicule. Nevertheless the parents soldiered on, going to the headmaster and defending their child's right to wear a dress at home. Meanwhile the child felt mortified and refused to wear that dress or any other. This is an example of an *inappropriate support*. Perhaps the child was Lunar type, amused by the clumsiness of the dress, or a Venus type, drawn to its colour and feel. Perhaps he was a Saturn type, interested in the experience of wearing something foreign to his usual clothing. Whatever, the *natural process* of experimenting and learning about life that was symbolized in the dress was blown out of proportion by the parents' well-intentioned but evidently clumsy interfering.

On the other end of the scale of parental support there is the couple with their child at a friend's house. The parents are warm, amiable, and completely unaware that their young child has encountered a cat for the first time, and is completely terrified. It takes another visitor to explain to the child, who is a Venus type, that the cat is friendly and harmless: the parents are completely unaware of the child's essence-type fears.

So when we think about understanding our children in the light of the differences brought about by different types, what should our attitude be?

- Firstly, to remember that we could be wrong, therefore to proceed cautiously.
- Secondly, that they have all the type-energies so the characteristics we detect may become central (indicating type) or be just a developmental phase.
- Thirdly, there may be other factors; loss, deprivation, trauma will all have an effect on the child, and their type characteristics may be disguised.

However, it is said that 'the child is father to the man' and it is unlikely, for example, that a child who is particularly kind in childhood (Jupiter and Lunar types) will grow up to be entirely brutal (deranged version of any type). A caveat here is that the child may be a Mars type who *was* delightful, up to the age when they went to school: outside the kindness of the home energy, the child may side with aggressive boys whose energy is a reflection of his own. Being delightful as a characteristic needs to survive the child going out into the school environment.

He or she may go through a 'rebellious' phase – which in type terms may be the action of a Mars type establishing their need for control. Contrarily, a Lunar type put under intense demands will possibly also rebel. The difference may be that the Mars type will remain under the parents' roof and negotiate their own power base, while the Lunar-type child may run away in order to experience independence.

Of course it would not be possible for us as parents or carers to avoid *any* kind of influence. Therefore our efforts are more likely to support and less likely to cause confusion if we observe the three tenets of the client-centred therapeutic approach, as defined by Carl Rogers: empathy, unconditional positive regard and congruence. The last is defined as the person in the 'therapist' position having their inner thought and feeling processes *available to their awareness*: if our child is breaking up the furniture, our congruence tells us to get them to stop, not celebrate their right to destroy.

Understanding Children Better by Changing Ourselves

The sub-heading here explains this idea. Yes, it is dangerous to decide what types our children are, and then to try to influence them in a particular direction, or shape their path. But it is possible for us to change ourselves in order to be better equipped for our children's types.

Take the example of a family where the Mars-type father sees nothing wrong with planning the scholastic and social activities of his children. On exposure to the 12-type Enneagram he comes to understand that his 'frisky puppy' energy is not as helpful as trying to get things right for his children. Tentatively coming to believe that his daughter is a Lunar type, he consciously explores Lunar type himself. He comes to understand why his standard operating behaviour is so frightening to his daughter, and so, in his relationship to her, he moves more into the influence of Jupiter-type behaviour.

Another example would be a Lunar-type mother who realizes that her instinctive 'make believe' home life is not working with her Saturn-type son. She works to come out of her self-involved SelfWorld, moving first to Venus type, to acquire the passion for helping, then to Mercury type for organizing and setting up a plan, then to Saturn type to experience for herself the way her son views life.

Any empathic communication between ourselves and others leads to an improvement in the understanding of both.

Should our original efforts not be successful – for example, if we have come to the tentative belief that our child is, for example, a Saturn–Mars type, but find the child is not responding to our modified approach in the way a Saturn–Mars type would – then we can drop our original tentative conclusion, and look for other indications. Therefore our approach is always 'child-centred': it is not for them to modify according to our beliefs, but for us to be flexible and sensitive and to structure and adjust our beliefs so as to benefit our child and the children whom we encounter, socially or professionally.

Some Individual Type Characteristics

My teacher writes:

> Lunar types are often the subject of bullying, especially from Mars types. The Lunar type can adapt by learning how to 'kill' the Mars type's aggressive urges. Also the Lunar type can use their own type to look amazingly innocent when they do terrible things, and the parents might blame the other children. Lunar types are often in such an isolated world in their mind that they can imagine almost anything about themselves – what the world sees, oddly, is of no interest to them. They think they see the Saturn-type 'truth'.
>
> Venus type gets satisfaction by manipulating the feelings of others; they are often admired by other schoolchildren because Venus type seem to always get whatever they want.
>
> Venus- and Jupiter-type children are sensitive to the feelings of others and learn how to empathize in ways the other types do not.
>
> Mercury type are quick/direct – not graceful, Mars are powerful – not graceful. Mercury types collect a lot of information, and think they 'understand' the way a Lunar or Saturn type would.

Saturn types provide great comic relief when they try to reach out to become 'graceful'. 'popular' or any of the characteristics of other types.

Mars types are often incredibly aggressive when they are trying to 'help' – which they often do (it gives them a sense of power, often in an extremely good way). But the Mars type has no concept that they are still being a 'rough' Mars, instead of a naturally caring Jupiter type.

Jupiter children tend to want to eat more (not always) and often grow chubby at an early age. They also live to 'feed' others. Jupiter type learns how to get satisfaction by adapting/manipulating the feelings of others to make the others feel better. They uniquely can often comfort others just by 'being' there. Jupiter types, even if they grow quite fat are still curiously graceful. Jupiter types often have a difficult time with other schoolchildren because the others do not value emotional subtlety and think that the gentle, loving nature of Jupiter type is fake (because the other types do not have it in their own nature). They see the Jupiter type as 'losers'.

Jupiter types, often, especially when they get old, still want to help, and go to live with their relatives or children believing they are being a help, when actually they are creating an extra burden because there is nothing they can do, and the person in need of help now must take care of someone else.

PART SIX

Positive Emotions and Negative Emotions

Chapter 15

So Now, Am I Cured?

Exposure to the 12-type Enneagram is obviously illuminating. It is not, however, an instant cure for any thoughts or behaviours that have been troubling you. If you have always been prone to anger or paranoia, or if your primary centre is your mind or your feelings, this will continue to be true about you. What may be beginning to change about you, what is beginning to develop, is your understanding that by being more aware of the ongoing internal and external pageant of life you can have more insight into why things are done in a particular way, and which essence energy you can consciously move to, to bring about a more satisfactory process or result. Providing, that is, that you make actual efforts. Theory that remains as such may be full of potential worth, but is profitless in practical terms.

It is also not the case that having some understanding of type-energies means that our emotions will automatically become positive. Just as each essence type has its own particular way of understanding the world and every aspect in it, so when the effects of negativity are at work, *each type expresses unhappiness in terms of its characteristics*. Therefore, not only can we predict and observe the specific ways in which the different essence energies react to stress, negativity and unfortunate incidents, we can also identify what is necessary to bring the person out of their spiral of negative type-led behaviour.

The 'Deadly' Aspect of each Essence Energy

Lunar type: Deadly Honesty

Description: The clear, simple way Lunar type views the world means that, even in a sophisticated adult individual, the type may on occasion speak or act in a way that others find naïve, inept or inappropriate. Even when the Lunar type knows, from past experience, that behaving in a particular way will *not* give them the result they want, they will continue to do so. They may explain this as 'I just have to do what I have to do.' They may secretly be proud of their 'honesty', yet they will suffer when they see how others react. They will also know that they should *not* tell the world everything about themselves and what they are doing. Yet they will also not be able to draw a line or curb their deadly honesty. They have a curiously over-developed and skewed sense of responsibility that leads them to agree to things that are nothing to do with them, or that put them in a difficult or invidious position. They promise things they should not, and then suffer trying to keep the promise ('I promise you I will protect you so no one ever discovers it was you who stole the money').

Cure: Move towards Venus type's self-protection. Let go of the notion that you have to speak out about everything you know. Do not see yourself as 'the one' who magically sorts out someone else's mess.

Venus type: Deadly Image-conscious

Description: The men who slap on after-shave, and wince at its sting, have bought the idea that beauty requires pain. Yet the only reason the lotion stings is that the manufacturer has added a skin irritant specifically so the hapless Venus type will feel it's 'doing some good'. Then there's the fashion victim who crushes her toes into unsuitable shoes, or walks around in a too-tight skirt or enormous heels. Of more serious concern are the Venus types who consider suicide as the logical answer to growing older, or who spend a great deal of money on dubious plastic surgery. Men who start using Botox in their twenties. Women who starve or purge themselves. Being slave to an image requires discipline but the rewards are often transitory and without real worth.

Cure: Let your hair down. Rejoice in the thought that how you look *really isn't that important*. Pursue goals outside of your own agenda.

Mercury type: Deadly Driven

Description: This type doesn't mine its own gold. They begin projects with promise but give up before taking the time needed to bring their efforts to fruition. With Venus-type energy in their past, they allot far too little time for romance. They develop a nervous 'that's me!' shrug when each attempt does not pan out, without slowing down to accept that they *could* have behaved differently. Over the years the sum total of this behaviour is the self-inflicted belief that 'Whatever I do it's not good enough.'

Cure: Accept that you have the ability to change your course. Think about cutting *in half* the easy-to-initiate projects. Learn to relax, physically and mentally; you are a 'moving' type but add thought to your actions. What is truly impressive is devoting real portions of your lives to a thoroughly grounded, well-conceived and properly executed project or relationship.

Saturn type: Deadly Serious

Description: Instead of retaining some Lunar-type lightness or fun, when Saturn types become deadly serious they smother the spark and insist on the driest of fact and behaviour. The Puritans wore deadly black and sinless white and there was no room for fun or life in between. Nowadays this is experienced in the behaviour of Saturn types who plod pedantically, arguing tiny, inconsequential issues with missionary zeal.

Cure: Learn to dance. Explore lightness and frivolity. Indulge without guilt. Recognize that not everything deserves the same seriousness. Forgive others for what you perceive as their shortcomings, shallowness or ignorance.

Mars type: Deadly Controlling

Description: The forceful charm and bold initiatives of this type can deteriorate into a life-or-death ego struggle. The naturally combative energy of this type easily becomes an ugly, endless confrontation. When lost in deadly control they would prefer that the house burn down rather than be blamed for not fitting a smoke alarm. The cumulative toll of years of over-intense engagement may rob this type of the golden years of retirement.

Cure: Learn to let go. Learn to consider the other, and to strive for win–win solutions. Develop the taste for being generous and all-embracing.

Jupiter type: Deadly Self-Sacrificing

Description: An over-identification with God in any form, or an over-developed sense of guilt involving personal penance, can lead to an ongoing personal creed of self-denial. The worker who walks rather than take a taxi the several miles to their next appointment and then does not buy themselves lunch on the company is not saving resources, they are burning themselves up and, eventually, out. The individual who lives in squalor while they pay the bills for people who could work perfectly well themselves is not 'saint-like'; they are being taken advantage of and the other side will one day walk away without a nod of thanks.

Cure: 'God helps those who help themselves.' In this context it means that saintly self-denial in the hope that you will be showered with supernatural gold is unwise. Helping others should begin from a platform of personal strength and security. Therefore work to establish yourself and you will see that you have *more* ability to help, not less.

Reading these descriptions, the hybrid types will recognize which of their two essence influences will be helped by following the 'cure'. Please also see 'A Note on Hybrid-Type Unhappiness' after the next section.

'Unhappiness' by Type: Form and Cure

Now we will explore how each main essence energy leads to a specific form of unhappiness for each type.

Lunar Type

Form of unhappiness: If this were an ideal world, the Lunar type would always be encouraged to manifest their type essence – childlike, charming, innocent. But, firstly, the world does not yet work in the light of this system. Secondly, our various life-demands cause this type to move away from their essence and towards one of the other type-energies. The Lunar type typically approaches the outside world with confidence and kindness, but when this is rebuffed they retreat into their internal world. They hit out as an expression of their inner pain, and pile on the aggression in the hope it will somehow turn off the pain.

If the negative situation continues, the Lunar type spirals into an exaggeration and magnification of their usual type characteristics. The Lunar type rejects offers of help from the outside because in their distress they believe it is better to be internally 'locked down'. They believe that exposing their terror and pain to the outside world, *and having the other side make an inadequate or unhelpful intervention,* is worse than coping on their own. For example, a Lunar type who has fallen down on their mortgage payments will not contact the bank or work out a payment plan with more organized friends. Instead they may take out further loans and quiet their inner anxiety by telling themselves that they will pay it all back when they win the Lottery. So as the spiral of unhappiness progresses, Lunar types both *isolate* when they should *communicate* and *fabricate* an unrealistic solution to their problems. As their grip on external reality further decreases their efforts may go towards elaborating on their fabrication, such as adding 'I will go to church every day for a year if God wins the lottery for me.'

By the time a Lunar type lets the outside world in, the situation has become completely unmanageable. Then the Lunar type turns to older types, to those they can turn into 'magic parents' or 'salvation'. However old they are, the undeveloped Lunar type is always on the look-out for those they can turn into 'best friends' or advisors, and if they have missed out on good parenting they will seek out couples, of any gender combination, and turn these into symbolic parents. They often get away with this because of their genuine charm but sometimes they have created such disaster that they can only face the painful consequences.

Cure: To face the consequences of their actions without running away or drowning in self-pity will always be an invaluable life lesson for the Lunar type. What is needed is for the Lunar type to *accept emotional responsibility,* both towards themselves and to others. To learn to see both themselves and the others as adults and individuals and not to seek to pursue an endless childhood. Some Lunar types have a particular problem with self-pity that does them no good. It makes them seek out scenarios in which they can be helpless and the object of sympathy when what they really need is to have their real strengths validated and supported.

Lunar types live intensely within their own inner world. What helps to restore harmony are inner and outer activities which give them perspective and balance. Exercises that train the mind, emotions and body. Counting exercises, children's games like 'Simon Says' or 'I Went to Market and I Bought', force the imagination to concentrate and remember specific details. Dance classes, where the Lunar type learns to bring together the mind and body, are excellent, although 'free expression' classes will not teach the desired discipline. Overall, accessing the benefits of Venus-type energy, particularly the energy's trait of *scrupulousness* can overcome the reckless Lunar-type imagination.

Venus Type

Form of unhappiness: Because appearance is so important in their value system, they can be happy only when they feel themselves well reflected in the opinions of others. Being far from the centre of intellectual thought and being one of the two *earth* types, they react to fleeting, valueless comments in their version of seriousness and, as a result, genuinely suffer. The need to compare well becomes a form of slavery. Being 'languorous' they always have to overcome their natural inertia. They deny themselves experiences, telling themselves it will be 'uncomfortable' because there will be wind, too much sun, too many ants, or whatever.

Secretly they long for someone to sweep them bodily out of their languor but since the type works *indirectly*, this is not communicated. In any case, the other side will not be a mind-reader or capable of the 'big gesture' they secretly crave. So the Venus type continues to read wildly romantic novels or watch addictive, agonized soaps where every moment is a drama and everyone talks obsessively and mechanically about feelings. In these scenarios the tiniest perceived slight is discussed as a matter of crucial importance and the undeveloped Venus type may attempt to live this kind of existence. The worse they feel, the more they cover their distress with a new haircut, clothes or expensive perfume.

They live 'down a well' where their sense of vanity flips into a sense of complete worthlessness and undesirability. This is made worse by an increasing need to pretend that all is perfect, which leads to their becoming arrogant and snobbish when they feel most vulnerable.

This type's reliance on the opinions of others causes them to doubt and ignore their own emotional intelligence. They struggle with their own version of a 'caste system' in which they can only be with people of similar loves, clothes, lifestyle.

They invest all their hopes in their physical appearance, so that the way they present themselves is also symbolic, a metaphor for their huge attraction to perfection. This can also lead to defeat because, once the other party has got through the armour of expensive haircut and impeccable clothes, the Venus type's generic thoughts (being one of the two 'earth' types, they see things in simple, concrete terms) can be an anti-climax. This is particularly unfortunate because the more unhappy the Venus type is, the more they will concentrate on winning a beautiful mate in order to feel better about themselves. And the more they will remain slaves to physical and financial appearances.

Cure: Clearly it would be helpful for the Venus type to find a way to step outside the gilded cage. Volunteering to help others would be especially beneficial. Seeing how others survive gives them perspective. What is most necessary is that they stop obsessing about 'perfection' and how they will 'let themselves down'. Being involved in creative pursuits helps as long as they don't turn this into a competition. 'Good enough' is a particularly desirable mindset to attain. Once the type can get casual, once they can let down their hair and not bother about appearances, they will become internally free. Then both they and others can enjoy their natural warmth and sensuousness.

Mercury Type

Form of unhappiness: Beneath Mercury type's busy-ness there is a fear. What will happen if I slow down? What thoughts of death and feelings of despair am I keeping at bay through busy-ness? This type is always on the lookout for new projects, new gimmicks, new opportunities – but these are often a distraction from the multitude of half-finished projects they already carry around.

Mercury types have an ongoing dissatisfaction with their lot. They attempt to solve this by looking for 'magic solutions'. These may be in the form of a particular song, a new job or indeed an entirely different way of looking at life. They thrive on the 'initial energy' of a project, but they are all too ready to slap together a generic rendition of the idea rather than invest proper time and commitment.

Occasionally, either because they are temporarily stuck or because their latest endeavour has come adrift, they stop for a moment and take stock. Then they judge themselves and fall easily into self-loathing for their unrealized activities. But this is obviously unpleasant, so they immediately renew their movements.

Cure: What helps Mercury type is to find a resting place somewhere between their usual frenetic behaviour and the opposite 'crashing'. They should be encouraged to work at 'half pace', which brings them into Venus-type territory. Here they can renew themselves in this type's emotional nurturing. Mercury types often believe they have got love 'licked', whereas they have a distant, cold attitude towards their partners. So it is desirable that they learn to love sincerely. Yoga and other activities that force them to bring their wayward movements into an inner discipline are helpful. They benefit from an outsider reviewing their various enterprises and formulating a plan for dealing with each project or interest. They will gain a sense of inner peace by helping without publicizing. Anonymous gestures of worthwhile help, especially focusing on helping others to love more deeply, lead this type to inner balance and happiness.

Saturn Type

Form of unhappiness: This type embraces both creativity and depression. They feel things intellectually, and sigh deeply as they pull their bodies through the day. For this type 'worth' is both the touchstone and a burden since everything needs to be questioned, evaluated, determined. They work at depth, in seclusion or isolation, driven on by a passion for the subject, but may become bitter at what they see as society's inability to understand and appreciate the fruits of their labour (they may labour on tiny adjustments, like a particular word, so what they produce has a sense of agony about it).

They are deeply troubled by people's words and actions because of a particularity of their type-energy. Because *they* seek worth and meaning in everything, they assume everyone else does as well. A careless Lunar-type comment will be examined for its 'secret meaning'. A thoughtless act will cause them intellectual agony because they do not stop to think whether or not the act was deliberate: they automatically assume it was and *do not question this*. The deep seriousness also leads them to cut themselves off from lightness and joy.

In the later stages of unhappiness this type pursues a path of self-destruction. Because there is unhappiness in the world they cannot feel happy. Instead they blame the world for not recognizing their worth, and deliberately shut down their admirable sense of worth in favour of cynical, world-weary disbelief in anything positive.

Cure: What helps is for this type to acknowledge that they cannot, through their efforts, bring the entire world up to a greater consciousness. Instead they need to re-awaken their own need for comfort and relief. Since we have all the type-energies inside us, by ruthlessly pursuing profundity and deep seriousness they are cutting themselves off from the gentler, lighter energies that are also a part of nature. Therefore they should study joy and the physical world and learn to integrate these concepts into their mental world. This type is admirably placed to learn new things: learning about healthy eating and exercise and discovering that not every conversation needs to be a tussle with conscience, morality, mortality and divine justice. They need to address the 'lower' tasks like eating properly, forcing themselves into regular exercise, and accepting that the world is as it is. By letting go of what has been unhelpful this type can embrace the truth: they are equipped better than any other type to understand and overcome their problems.

Mars Type

Form of unhappiness: In positive mode, this type is dynamic and draws people into their orbit. However, emotionally speaking they experience their affect as liable to change, and paranoically suspect others of doing the same thing. They seem confident but they may ask 'How am I doing?' as though they have a sense of putting energy out but needing external validation. The rookie employee may be surprised when the boss asks 'Did I do that right?' Being one of the two 'movement' types they have a restless need to 'do something' in order to shore up their self-opinion.

Although they may seem powerful, their inner vacillation and need for a fight is wearing on them too. Then they want everything to be 'wonderful'. They buy presents to make things better, like the businessman buying his neglected wife jewellery, but when this doesn't do the trick they revert to aggression. Yet they are still hurting, although they cannot show vulnerability. If the Mars type cannot step out of type blindness they need the other side to draw the line. So they push people, often intuitively hoping the other side will stand up for themselves. If the other side does, then the Mars type will happily relax, enjoying not always having to be the one who makes the decision or the threat. Sometimes they will alienate family, friends and business associates. This is actually disturbing for the Mars type because they long for harmony, respect and a 'magic solution', a 'search for Camelot', while desperately thinking 'This is it/This time I'll win.' Unfortunately they usually pick an unrealistic 'childish' solution. When this doesn't work out, they may walk down the street wanting to fight someone or even everyone.

Cure: What helps is to surround this type with accepting, generous, Jupiter-type love. The constant warrior needs time to bathe and lick his or her wounds. When they are riding high this will seem unthinkable, ludicrous. But reaching out with unconditional love to the Mars type at the right moment leads to their retiring from the fight. They are also helped by learning to trust that *they are okay* rather than unconsciously following the constant need to pit themselves against others and life. This type often becomes involved in charitable or other productive, non-competitive work where they can use their talents for organization and management for the greater good.

Jupiter Type

Form of unhappiness: This type wants desperately to believe that things will be all right in the world. They lie to themselves and others because the truth about life is too difficult. They have a belief that there is a 'saviour' somewhere who will bring peace to them and the world. The dopy Jupiter type, perhaps overly impacted by the ills of the world, may develop a mechanical 'that's terrible' response to everything rather than actually doing what they can to change and improve things. Others see them as suffering for the universe while inside they may actually be *feeling sorry for themselves*. They will neglect their true needs and indulge themselves in unnecessary pain. They may take a perverse delight in breaking up with someone because they can use it as an opportunity to say that they don't have any emotional needs; everything is for 'others'. Having denied their needs and disappointed those who offered them love, they may take refuge in conventional religion or mystics and wait for 'salvation'.

Cure: Instead of idly waiting for revelation and sanctification, the Jupiter type gains by accomplishing small, real, tasks that suit the energy's home-loving orientation. Rather than beginning a homily with 'As I was saying to Jesus this morning' the type benefits from putting the principles of the saints into effect – while not believing that they themselves are 'saintly'. Focusing on cleaning up around them and being 'good householders' is particularly rewarding for this type. As is asking their internal 'wise father' (Santa Claus is a Jupiter type) what they *can* do and then simply making the effort, stripped of 'mystical' intentions. They are also helped by drawing a line under suffering and giving themselves over to lightness. This type finds happiness by nurturing themselves with things that they could otherwise feel guilty for doing.

A Note on Hybrid-Type Unhappiness

My teacher writes 'The hybrid types are vulnerable because their split nature can pull them apart. Conversely, they can use both type energies to their advantage. An example is the actress Jean Seberg, who certainly used both Lunar and Venus rays to her advantage, but in the end they pulled her apart. The Lunar never quite knowing who she was or where she fitted in, the Venus knowing she could attract anyone but couldn't maintain the kind of relationship she needed. There are many hybrid types who managed both types just fine – for example Barbara Stanwyck (Saturn–Mars type).'

Chapter 16

More on Identifying Types – And a Warning

Author's Note: If we mentally revisit and review the different subjects, layers of meaning, and aspects of exploration presented in the different chapters, we have an impression of enormous depth, intensity and volume. It is something of this that we need to hold in our awareness when seeking to identify which type may be our 'essence type'.

In answer to a question I asked, my teacher wrote to me specifically about 'recognizing your type':

> In my experience, people cannot see about themselves what is perfectly obvious to everybody else. It helps to have a class situation where an obvious Mercury type is on the stage arguing that they are a Saturn type. When 15 or more people suddenly cry out 'No, you're not seeing . . .!' it helps. I think you could easily explore [in this book] the idea that everyone has the characteristics of every type, but only one type has them as a way of life. All types can be bold, but the world recognizes who is a Mars type and who is just bold on occasion. The world recognizes the gentle otherworldly childlike nature that is 'natural' for a Lunar type, and when other types play at being that type they fall short.
>
> Once in class . . . I left the room and completely wet my head with water to illustrate a point. When I came back in the room everyone was arguing whether or not I had proved the point (whatever it was), until one woman, a Jupiter type, said to me, very loudly and pointedly, 'Go dry your hair. You'll catch a cold.' Suddenly a Venus-type woman said 'You see, I don't believe that's real. I think

that's fake concern.' The Jupiter type again said 'Go dry your hair.' And I began to understand the real point of the argument.

I started to talk about the 'small' side of the 12-type Enneagram [Lunar, Venus and Mercury types] and how they couldn't see the world except through the narrow lens of 'self'. The 'large' side [Saturn, Mars and Jupiter types], by default, concentrate on 'out there', on the 'other person'. The Venus-type woman later told me it was one of the most important lessons of her life. She was ashamed that she had dared question the sincerity of a class member, and she was embarrassed that the Jupiter-type woman hadn't even noticed that someone was insulting her.

Correspondence with my teacher is always a great joy and a privilege to me. We can see how much valuable instruction he includes in a few sentences. Here there is the comment that 'everyone has the characteristics of every type, *but only one type has them as a way of life*' (my italics). This is the reason why we gain by taking general concepts and examining them in the light of what we know about the different types. My teacher's examples are the boldness of Mars type (which other types will access accidentally, or, after exposure to the 12-type Enneagram, can access consciously) and the genuinely childlike SelfWorld of the Lunar type (which is also readily accessed by Jupiter type going forward, by Saturn type by choice and default, and with a more self-asserting version in the default of Mars type).

There is no judgement attached to being one type or another. Yet, as was realized by the Venus-type woman in my teacher's anecdote, the differences between types are *real*. Venus and Venus–Mercury types may be attracted to, say, the church or social work or what they perceive as a 'helping' path, because of the 'glamour' of helping, and not understand that the concern of Saturn, Mars–Jupiter and Jupiter types for others is *real*, not 'fake concern'. Here it is not necessary for the smaller types to forgo areas where they can experience the larger-type concerns, only that they seek to discover for themselves the same deep responses to the concept of concern for others that would be natural to one of the larger, or older, types.

So, when determining our own type, again we bear in mind the image of the gun being loaded. Particularly we bear in mind my teacher's note that *others can see who we are better than we can ourselves*. This is because each type has type-blindness. Some of our type characteristics will not be valued, and even dismissed. For example, Lunar types cannot understand why some other types aren't 'kind' like they are, a trait they don't attach much importance to since it is how they operate naturally. Saturn types cannot understand why other people don't question everything. Jupiter types cannot understand why other people are not concerned for others living somewhere else. By making a list of our characteristics, and those of others, we will be more able to identify who is which essence type.

Focusing on Identifying Our Type

So we bear in mind that others can often see our 12-type Enneagram type better than we can – at least to start with. Once we have heard, read or recognized, and genuinely believe, which type we are, it is *enormously comforting and grounding*, even if we are a type we are not drawn to. I recall a woman in my teacher's school saying she just had to accept that she *was* a Jupiter type, when she really wanted to be a self-obsessed Venus type because it would be easier: however begrudgingly, she *was* accepting her destiny. Here the power is of knowing the base from which we must start. And of course, if there are aspects of your type that you do not like, it will obviously be beneficial for you to recognize these as *type characteristics*, so you can consciously work to influence and modify them ('changing' them in a radical way may be beyond your ability: we have to work with the characteristics we have been given).

Finally, when the chips are down, cards are on the table and the masks are removed – there we are. 'Jupiter' types are revealed as Mars types, frantic 'Mercury' types are seen to be chaotic Lunar types, and so on. If we remember that the principal purpose of our lives from the 12-Type Enneagram perspective is to *learn how to be a good* (evolved and more conscious) *representative of our type*, we can finally accept that being who we are is more important than being what others want us to be, or even what would be most convenient, from a work or love-life perspective.

Please refer back to the Type Identification test at the end of Chapter 5.

Repeating the Type Identification Warning

This is always the same, the image of *the gun in the process of being loaded*. In other words, the gun is not already loaded, it is a process in which we are involved. By opening our eyes to the 12-type Enneagram we are also accepting the *responsibility* for getting the information right. It is an esoteric truth that it is better *not* to progress spiritually than to develop *in the wrong way/direction* (and if we have been on the receiving end of manic religious fervour we may already understand the wisdom of this remark). It is the same with the 12-type Enneagram: it is better just to read the book and think of it as interesting information and leave it there rather than to decide that we are one type or another and shoehorn our psyche into what may become a straitjacket. And not even the right straitjacket for our essence type.

However, the usual experience of exposure to the 12-type Enneagram is that people readily understand why other people think they are one type or another, and once people have accustomed themselves to the descriptions and the other information as set down in this book, they are able to decide for themselves where they might be. As we move through the world with greater knowledge of the Enneagram, we find ourselves asking the questions 'Where am I now in terms of my 12-type Enneagram energy?' 'At what rate (beats per minute) am I operating?' so we can then be properly informed and take advantage of the system's myriad applications.

As throughout the book, the ideas above are *impressions* of how the various type-energies may manifest. Once you have formed a tentative opinion of someone's essence type, compare the observations you have made with what you know about them. Or observe someone in the light of unhappiness for all the types, and see which pattern they fall into.

Throughout the book, the major organizational themes have been to present the information offered by my teacher, then to interpret and bring to life this information through everyday examples. In this way the knowledge, which is of 'higher' origin, can be made accessible to us in our daily lives, the way Christ used parables to convey important lessons and teachings.

Two Further Lists of Type Characteristics

Different Types of Energy

We are already aware that each type has particular characteristics. There is also a specific type of energy employed by each type:

Lunar type:	Star energy
Venus type:	Water energy
Mercury type:	Air energy
Saturn type:	Earth energy
Mars type:	Fire energy
Jupiter type:	Sun energy

- Other-worldly **Lunar type** is nurtured by star energy. We can see how the type's sense of isolation, of living remotely in their own world, and their immediate attraction to shiny objects and bright colours fits.
- **Venus type**'s water energy reminds us of the languid, flowing, sensuous movements of the type: imagine water pouring gently down a pebbled stream. Water does not confront, it flows around resisting objects, which ties in with this type's indirect, subtle manipulative approach.
- We can picture **Mercury type**'s air energy in their relentless moving around, like air currents that throw birds one way and then another. It is fast and un-anchored, mirrored in this type's constant jumping from one topic to the next.
- The earth energy of **Saturn type** we visualize as giving us all a solid foundation. We imagine the depths of caves, endless desert and inaccessible mountain landscapes. From this we draw together an image of this type's enormously far-reaching vision and intellectual span.
- That **Mars type**'s energy is fire is fascinating. Here we think of the profound power of fire, and how it can have enormous influence from the warmth of a log fire to the devastation of a forest fire.
- We can draw an analogy between **Jupiter**'s energy and the idea of the sun shining down on the earth, providing

warmth and light, and making no distinction between those who 'deserve' sunshine, and those who do not. In just this way the Jupiter type offers their warmth and lack of criticism to the world.

Different Energies: Hybrid Types

There are no specifically different energies for the hybrid types. They have the dual influence of the main types.

Lunar–Venus type:	Star and water energy
Venus–Mercury type:	Water and air energy
Mercury–Saturn type:	Air and earth energy
Saturn–Mars type:	Earth and fire energy
Mars–Jupiter type:	Fire and sun energy
Jupiter–Lunar type:	Sun and star energy

- The combination of star and water for the **Lunar–Venus type** helps to clarify why this type is the most vulnerable. Star energy is a long way away; water is not capable of standing up to some pressures.
- The **Venus–Mercury type** hybrid needs to think of the earth in which water flows, the air that hovers over the ground, and try to ensure they ground their influences in stable earth (i.e. thinking also).
- **Mercury–Saturn type**'s combination of air and earth offers the type a choice: stay on the surface or take advantage of being earth-rooted.
- Earth and fire influences underline **Saturn–Mars type**'s bold striving for personally focused societal achievement.
- **Mars–Jupiter type**'s combination of fire and sun energy explains the type's extraordinary resilience and determination.
- Possession of both sun and star energy highlights **Jupiter–Lunar type**'s combination of larger and smaller energy.

Symbols Associated with the Essence Types

There is so much detail and breadth in the knowledge contained in the 12-type Enneagram. Here is another example: each energy also has a particular animal or other symbol.

Lunar type:	Birds
Venus type:	Fish
Mercury type:	Ants
Saturn type:	Man
Mars type:	Reptiles
Jupiter type:	Sun

- We recognize **Lunar type**'s birdlike, quick, 'pecking' movements. We think of the customary fragility of a bird, but we also think of birds of prey and remember that this type can, in danger or fear, become fierce.
- At first the idea that sensuous **Venus type**'s symbol is the fish seems odd – surely fish are cold and slimy? But then we think of the fish gliding through reeds, going with the flow of the current, and we recognize the Venus type's indirect, subtle manipulation of their environment.
- **Mercury types** may not like the idea of ants being their symbol, but they will have to agree that the idea of hundreds, or thousands, of creatures busily carrying out their tasks *does* remind them of their constant flow of activities.
- That **Saturn type**'s symbol is man itself suggests that the Saturn-type approach to life is the most becoming. This is the energy that is most concerned with understanding the why and how of life and when we are in this energy we seriously actualize our human potential. (*'Man' of course also includes 'woman' and 'child' here.*)
- **Mars types** may not appreciate that their symbol is the reptile. Yet this fact is not only a tribute to their toughness, it is an indication to the rest of us how carefully the type needs to be treated.
- Seeing that **Jupiter type**'s energy is the sun, it can seem repetitive that their symbol is also the sun. Yet if we remember that without the sun we have nothing then we appreciate the all-importance of the sun in our lives, and we take Jupiter's symbol as informing us just how valuable this type is in our lives, and why we should support and value them.

Different Symbols: Hybrid Types

Again there are no separate symbols for the hybrid types, but they have dual influences.

Lunar–Venus type:	Bird and fish
Venus–Mercury type:	Fish and ants
Mercury–Saturn type:	Ants and man
Saturn–Mars type:	Man and reptiles
Mars–Jupiter type:	Reptiles and sun
Jupiter–Lunar type:	Sun and bird

- Both birds and fish, the symbols associated with the **Lunar–Venus type**, are vulnerable and hunted by other species.
- Fish and ants give us **Venus–Mercury type**'s fascinating combination of indirectness and speed.
- Ants and man, the combination associated with **Mercury–Saturn type**, is again a challenge for the type: will they remain in the dirt, or take their proper place as the prime species?
- That man and reptiles are associated with **Saturn–Mars type** is interesting because it highlights the type's place between the lower and higher order: which side will they choose?
- Reptiles and sun, the symbols associated with **Mars–Jupiter type**, explain the type's tough impregnable skin (and lack of interest in their own comfort) while they spread their inner sunshine.
- Sun and bird, associated with the **Jupiter–Lunar type**, give us insight into the great warmth and also the charm and vulnerability of this hybrid.

In the final section of the book we will use the information we have learned to apply the wisdom of the 12-type Enneagram to our lives and the lives of everyone we know.

PART SEVEN

Taking the 12-Type Enneagram Into Our World

Chapter 17

Working with the 12-Type Enneagram

Astrology? The 12-Type Enneagram?

My teacher writes: 'Planetary rays from the planets themselves are the subject of astrology – dealing with influences coming from *the outside*. The whole point of the 12-type Enneagram is that we recognize that the more important planetary influences come from *inside us*. Moreover, planetary influences from the outside happen when planets are in certain positions with respect to other planets, and so on. It is obvious that our problems and our opportunities are mostly *not* periodic, that things happen because of where Mercury or Saturn are at the moment. Rather our problems and opportunities come from our inner state of *being* and have to do with how well we have adjusted to our inner planetary existence and how well we manage the essence-type forces of the people around us.'

Real-Life Scenarios

So let us begin to work with the system. The following imagined dialogues are taken from real-life scenarios. Dialogues are a good way of learning how to introduce the knowledge of the 12-type Enneagram into everyday situations. As always, we would want to do this with respect for both the system and the person to whom we are talking.

Scenario

You realize your brother is probably a Mars type. You know he rejects criticism. He has just spent the last ten minutes telling you what he is going to say to his boss in the morning. You are worried that his anger is going to create an unfortunate confrontation. You are also aware that when your brother gets into a confrontation he blows up. Previously he lost a job because he just walked out.

> **You:** Can you help me?
>
> **Brother:** What?
>
> **You:** There's something I want to ask you. But I don't know how to do it.
>
> **Brother:** Just tell me.
>
> **You:** Okay. I'm concerned that when you speak to your boss tomorrow you will be so angry that you won't put your points across in such a way that he will hear them. I think he will definitely get that you are angry. But he won't see that you have a legitimate argument. I'm concerned that you won't be able to get your side of the story across.
>
> **Brother:** That's his problem.
>
>   (Silence)
>
>   What?
>
> **You:** I have to be cautious here. I want to agree with you. But I also know you basically enjoy your job. I wonder what you can do to get your issues across without letting the anger out?
>
> **Brother:** He's the boss. It's his job to listen.
>
>   (Silence)
>
> **You:** He's also the boss.
>
>   (Silence)
>
> **Brother:** What do you think I should do?
>
> **You:** I think you have real points to get across. Maybe if you worked out exactly what you need to say. Rehearse it. Shout at me. But don't shout at him. Get your points across.

'You' begins with the knowledge of his brother's type. 'You' is using a Jupiter-type approach that disarms by being balanced and respectful. Note the use of silence when the brother makes an aggressive statement. Finally the brother is ready to listen to another way of approaching the issue. By repetition, 'You' underlines the principal task: 'Don't get angry and fail to get your points across.'

Scenario

'You' are the husband. Your wife, you believe, is a Venus type. She used to work at a bank but she was made redundant. Since then she lies around the house watching trash TV. She cries when you talk about her looking for work. You are concerned that she is going deeper into a spiral of depression. She refuses to see her doctor because she says taking anti-depressants is bad for you.

You: I'll be home about seven.

Wife: I'll be here. Of course. Where else would I be?

You: I like the thought of your being here when I get home.

Wife: I'm so bored.

(Silence)

And don't tell me to look at the jobs on the Internet. All they want is young girls. I'm never going to work again.

(Silence)

Why aren't you talking to me?

You: I am. I just don't know what to say when you talk like that. You are a lovely, intelligent woman.

Wife: So find me a job.

You: I've tried. You didn't like my suggestions.

Wife: You don't know how discouraged I am.

You: Tell me.

(Pause)

Wife: I hate having to run around all the time. I wake up dreading the day ahead.

You: Remember the book I read about the Enneagram? You know I said I thought you were a Venus type. Venus types are great to be around, they're warm and caring. But their energy is pretty slow. I understand that the running around tires you out. What I suggest is you look for a job where you can do things in your own time.

Wife: That sounds perfect but where do I find it?

You: Why don't you tell me?

Wife: What?

You: I know being made redundant knocked your confidence. But I also know what you can do. You can run around like the young girls. Maybe not all the time, but a few hours a day. I know you can.

Wife: So what are you telling me?

You: Not telling you. I'm saying that you *can* organize your life. I've seen you. So why don't you do this? Every day, just do three things towards getting a job.

Wife: What three things?

You: Any three things you like. Spend half an hour on the computer seeing what's out there. Walking down the high street to see if anyone's hiring. Call anyone who might know someone who's got an opening.

Then you can watch TV. You'll have earned it.

'You' uses a mixture of Jupiter-type and Saturn-type energy. 'You' speaks from understanding his wife's slower-moving Venus-type energy. He also knows that Venus types, when they get knocked, tend to spiral down into themselves. They quickly feel helpless. So he suggests the 'three things a day' approach, which is simple and effective. He also reminds her that, although her confidence has been knocked, she can run around, just not all the time. So he indicates a cut-off point, and suggests the same activity she has been doing, watching TV, but now as a reward, not a way to fill in dead time.

Scenario

'You' need to break up with your boyfriend. You have realized that he is a Saturn type. You are a Venus–Mercury type. Although you enjoy that he makes you think more deeply, he is so mired in Saturn-type seriousness that he's smothering your type-need to have fun. When you try to talk to him he defaults into negative Mars-type energy and tells you if you don't like it, leave. Your last relationship ended badly so you want to use the Enneagram to bring this relationship to an ending that is less damaging for you.

You: You know how you always tell me I'm not serious enough?

Boyfriend: Uhuh?

You: I have never been more serious than right now.

Boyfriend: I'm glad to hear it.

You: Don't be glad. I'm sorry to say that I think we should break up.

Boyfriend: *What?*

You: I'm not making a drama. I don't want you to talk me out of it. Let's talk about it as adults.

Boyfriend: What if I don't want you to break up with me?

You: That would be kind of you to say so but it's not your choice.

Boyfriend: Why are you being so hostile?

You: What have I said that's hostile?

Boyfriend: Everything. You're acting like my mother.

You: Your mother is a Mars type. I am a Venus–Mercury type. We are not the same.

Boyfriend: When did you get so scary?

You: When being nice gave you permission to walk all over me.

Boyfriend: So why didn't you tell me?

You: I did. But I told you nice and you ignored me.

Boyfriend: So it's my fault?

(Silence)

Okay, this is interesting. Give me some pointers. How do you want me to speak to you?

You: You are so intelligent. You know more than I do about how you should speak to me.

(Pause)

Boyfriend: Okay. So where do we go from here?

You: We step away from each other. And go our own ways.

Boyfriend: I can't believe you are breaking up with me. And you do sound like my mother.

You: Interesting. So that's why you constantly put me down. You as a Saturn type have been defaulting to Lunar type. You become the child and make me the critical mother.

(Silence)

Boyfriend: I guess you're saying that's not a good thing.

You: I'm saying a lot of things. One of them is goodbye.

Prior to this conversation, 'You' has used the Enneagram to understand the basic incompatibility: the boyfriend keeps crushing her spirit. So she adopts a positive Mars-type energy. When he defaults into Lunar type ('How do you want me to speak to you?') she reminds him of his intelligence. She does not attack him. When he says she reminds him of his mother she does not react to the criticism, she thinks it through and realizes what he has been doing. We must imagine that in the break-up previous to this one 'You' did not stand up for herself. Here she remains in control throughout, and leaves the relationship on what for her is a positive note. This is a good example of a constructive use of Mars-type energy.

Scenario

'You' are a good friend of someone who needs the right kind of feedback. You believe they are a Lunar–Venus type. You know that they will run away from any sort of advice and deliberately, recklessly, continue the destructive behaviour.

> **You:** Who do you identify with more: Marilyn Monroe or Nicole Kidman.
>
> **Friend:** Marilyn of course, how can you even ask me that?
>
> **You:** What don't you like about Nicole?
>
> **Friend:** She's hard.
>
> **You:** So let's put the two women together: Marilyn was a divine, child-like woman. She made a great deal of money for other people. She was addicted to pills. She was abused in relationships. She married two men who didn't understand her. And eventually she died at 36. Nicole is an Oscar-winning actress. She makes millions of dollars a year both from films and prestigious advertising. She has been married for many years now to a handsome singer. Her 'yes' can get a movie made. If she's hard, perhaps you have to be hard to succeed.
>
> **Friend:** I could never be hard.
>
> **You:** But life is hard.
>
> **Friend:** Then I don't want to be alive.
>
> **You:** So kill yourself.
>
> **Friend:** How can you tell me that!
>
> **You:** I didn't. You did.
>
> **Friend:** Why are you picking on me?
>
> **You:** In terms of the 12-type Enneagram you are the Lunar–Venus type, 'The Sexy, Affectionate Childlike Adult'. So was Marilyn. So your identification is accurate. It's just *not helping you*.
>
> **Friend:** What do you want me to do about it?
>
> **You:** Your best protection is to understand your essence type. To understand what it makes you do. When you make a mess of things, it's often because you have been defaulting to undeveloped, unhelpful Lunar–Venus type energy. *But you don't have to*. The best thing for your type is to progress towards pure Venus type.
>
> **Friend:** Venus?

You: That's where we go for *emotional responsibility*. Venus types are meticulous in emotional and sexual situations. They don't let the guy or woman mess them around.

Friend: That would be a change for me.

You: Keep thinking 'emotional responsibility'. What is emotionally responsible for me? How can I be emotionally responsible in this situation? You can even write it down and next time we meet, rather than your telling me about the latest disaster, you could tell me about how you took emotional responsibility in some situations.

Clearly, 'You' has had enough of the Lunar–Venus type's perpetually messy relationship scenarios. 'You' begins by defining two very different women. Then 'You' lays down the most basic under-standing for the Lunar–Venus type: consciously to seek 'emotional responsibility'. The Lunar and to a lesser extent the Lunar–Venus type usually respond well to having their essence type explained. As 'childlike adults' they welcome information to understand themselves better. They also respond well to specific instructions.

Scenario

'You' are at a party. You are excited to see that also at the party is someone you have long admired, someone whose outspoken and selfless dedication to a political cause has brought you to regard them as a Mars–Jupiter type. You see their face looks exceedingly careworn. You see their nails are untrimmed and their trousers are faded. You appreciate that they are not interested in personal grooming but you also have an impression that they are slowly killing themselves.

You: Excuse me. I would like to talk to you for a couple of minutes.

Humanitarian: This seat is free.

You: This is a great moment for me.

Humanitarian: Oh please –

You: Have you heard of the 12-type Enneagram?

Humanitarian: I've heard of the Enneagram but I thought there were nine types.

You: This is a different system. It is concerned with what we call alchemical 'essence energy'. Each of the energies has the name of a planet. But it's not spacy. It's very specific. And in terms of the 12-type Enneagram, you are the Mars–Jupiter type, defined as humanitarians: 'forceful benevolence'.

Humanitarian: I don't like the idea of my fitting into a category.

You: I hate to say this and I hope it doesn't offend you. But that's the Mars-type energy speaking. Mars type is defined as the athlete-warrior. Well you are a warrior. But you're also the Jupiter type and they're defined as 'jolly, feeding parents'.

(Humanitarian laughs)

You: Please can I explain just one thing?

Humanitarian: You've come this far.

You: Part of the way in which the Mars–Jupiter type operates is that the person pays little heed to the importance of their own comfort or well-being. This is how Gandhi could use self-starvation to get people to listen to him. And I can see that you also are uninterested in your own well-being. But here's the question for me. How can you do all the good that you do, and *also* take care of yourself? I see you looking so tired and worn out. I want you to live for many years. I'm worried you won't last.

(Humanitarian laughs again)

Humanitarian: I'm indestructible. I don't have to look after myself.

You: But you remember Saint Francis on his deathbed asking his body for forgiveness for all the ill treatment he gave it?

Humanitarian: We have to do what we do.

You: But you *don't*. The 12-type Enneagram always gives the solution. And for the Mars–Jupiter, so they don't burn themselves out, it's to go towards the Lunar type: childlike, charming, innocent, trusting. Anything you can do that lifts your spirits and gives your body a little time to recover from the relentless battle of life. Another Mars–Jupiter type I know takes clown lessons!

Humanitarian: And I listen to music.

You: Great.

Humanitarian: But I suppose I could listen to something lighter. Once upon a time I liked jazz but I gave up because it seemed frivolous.

You: Yes. Frivolous is good!

(Humanitarian laughs again)

'You' is speaking in Lunar-type energy. It's disarming. The Humanitarian is used to more profound types. 'You' uses just enough argument with the St Francis reference to engage the Humanitarian more deeply. The Humanitarian laughs three times. Each time indicates an unbending, making him finally open to hearing about the 12-type Enneagram without engaging the denying Mars-type energy. What the Humanitarian will do with this moment is unknown. But 'You' has the satisfaction of contributing something of more potential worth than the usual 'I think you're wonderful.'

Scenario

How do you give feedback to your boss? It is not the case that all bosses are Mars type. It is true that the boss or authority figure, whatever their essence type, may have learned to operate somewhat in their own essence type's understanding of Mars type. In this scenario, the issue is that the Mercury type boss is under-performing on her management functions.

Boss: I don't have time to talk to you. I have six crises to sort out.

You: Talk to me. I'm your assistant.

Boss: It will take me longer to explain to you than to do it.

You: But I have read the same papers as you. Give me half.

Boss: I can't.

You: I suggest – (*you take up the papers and divide her workload into what you can deal with, what she can deal with.*)

Boss: (*Reluctantly*) Well come to me if you have a problem.

You: Can I say something?

Boss: If you must.

You: Does it make sense to you if I say that often I wish you only had half the number of projects. Because I think you would really like to do them all justice but it's always rushed.

Boss: It's the nature of our work.

You: But I was hired so you could delegate and concentrate on the more important issues.

Boss: They're all important!

You: Can I say something else?

Boss: If you must.

You: I just don't think that's true. But I think you *give* everything the *same* total importance.

Boss: Tell me why I do this?

You: It's in the 12-type Enneagram. You are a Mercury type. You use speed rather than any other energy. The reason why you give everything the same importance is you aren't *thinking first*.

Boss: I don't have time to think!

It will take more than one conversation for this boss to appreciate how she can approach her workload differently. The 12-type Enneagram essentially defines the problem and also gives 'You' the right tools for tackling the work.

How to Select the Right Energy for Each Situation

When we default, either into our own essence energy or to the type we have unconsciously defaulted to, we are using the energy blindly, mechanically. Selecting the right energy for a situation involves:

- Being aware of our own essence type.
- Being aware of where we would unconsciously default to, to deal with a situation.
- Evaluating the situation from the other person's point of view. Identifying their essence type. Predicting how their type will cause them to behave.
- Finally selecting the right energy for dealing with the situation.

Scenario

Let's call you 'John' and you are on holiday. During the day you have played an informal game of water polo with other hotel guests. One of the guests is a powerful, muscular man called 'Matt' to whom you have chatted casually. In the evening you see him with his girlfriend, supping pints of lager. You walk over and greet them with a friendly smile and are taken aback by Matt's totally unexpected, aggressive attitude.

Matt: You! You're in for trouble tomorrow.

John: Me? Why?

Matt: You're going to get it.
John: What have I done wrong?
Matt: You're nothing but trouble and you're going to pay.
John: But it's water polo. That's how you play it.
Matt: I'm going to get you!

Afterwards you consider the situation. You decide that Matt is a Mars type. You reflect on your playing. You remember that you were the one scoring goals for your team while Matt was somewhere playing defence. Somehow he has taken your scoring the goals personally and is not feeling in control. He is feeling marginalized and the aggression reflects his need to be in charge.

There are several ways you as John can respond, each time by going into (his particular essence-type version) of specific types.

Lunar type: Here John would simply avoid the water polo games from now on.
Venus type: This manipulative, indirect, subtle manner of working could be helpful. We will come back to this.
Mercury type: John would use *movement* to stay out of the man's way. Throughout the game he would need to know where Matt was at all times and stay out of his physical reach.
Saturn type: John would attempt to argue Matt intellectually into a more reasonable frame of mind.
Mars type: Aggression would be answered with aggression. John would hammer home points on how to play casual water polo in a holiday milieu.
Jupiter type: John would *selflessly* attempt to create a win–win situation.

In the actual incident that took place, John chose a combination of Venus and Jupiter-type energies. Not because he was afraid, but because he wanted to prove to himself how useful knowing Enneagram energies is in dealing with an actual incident.

John decided the best approach was a combination of Venus-type manipulation and Jupiter-type generosity. Seeing Matt later in the evening, rather than ignore him he spoke to him as though they were old friends, consciously accessing Jupiter type. Matt was brusque but John completely ignored this, empowered by

Jupiter type's lack of self-consciousness, and declared that the following day he would make sure he was on the same side as Matt.

The next day John chose a half-way position and persuaded Matt to tackle the other side's goal. John ensured that every time he had the ball he would pass it to Matt. Matt was not a great water polo player, but since he got the ball so often, he was able to score some points. Each time Matt scored John led the cheering.

Afterwards, seeing Matt with his girlfriend, John set the tone for how the situation would play by greeting them as though they were long-established friends: 'Here's the star of today's game. You were fantastic!' Since Matt was enjoying John's seemingly fawning behaviour, he was not likely to be aggressive. Matt relaxed in what seemed to be John's wholehearted admiration.

In fact, John was proving how easy Matt is to manipulate. Had John gone into Mars-type energy, with the type's preference for being on top, the two would have been caught in a spiral of hostility. By going into Jupiter type John lost the need to top Matt directly; instead he won by disarming him. He enjoyed the game *and* the experience of consciously using the two essence energies most advantageous in the situation.

This holiday anecdote involved a very simple scenario, but how would working consciously with the type-energies influence a much more complicated and significant situation?

Scenario

Pamela C is an international political strategist and trouble-shooter. She is the last-minute replacement for a diplomat who has taken ill. Pamela's brief is to keep the pot bubbling but make no promises of any sort. She meets the other four delegates. In the first few minutes of polite conversation it emerges:

> One is a Mars type
> One is a Mars–Jupiter type
> One is a Jupiter type
> One is a Mercury–Saturn type.

Each requires a different focus.

- She needs to prove to the Mars type that she is not just a temporary, powerless caretaker.
- She needs to form a temporary alliance with the Mars–Jupiter type.
- She needs to prevent the Jupiter type's need to please undermining her position.
- She needs to get the Mercury–Saturn type to focus on the issues that are important to *her*.

Conscious that she is a last-minute step-in, Pamela needs to use her knowledge of the 12-type Enneagram to bridge her lack of knowledge concerning the issue under scrutiny. The conversation might go like this:

Pam: Ambassador Briggs is ill. I will be speaking for him today and tomorrow.

Mars: I don't know your face.

Pam: I usually work behind the scenes. My security clearance is the same level as Ambassador Briggs'.

Jupiter: Please send the Ambassador my condolences.

Mars–Jupiter: And mine.

Mercury–Saturn: Why don't we club in for a fruit basket?

Pam: Thank you for your concern. I would imagine we have three items for discussion:

> The size of grant we are considering;
> The time frame;
> Monitoring progress to completion.

Have I included everything?

Mercury–Saturn: Isn't that enough?

Mars: As far as I'm concerned it's all about the size of grant.

Mars–Jupiter: We need to be cognizant of the number of people we can reach.

Pam: I agree (smiles warmly at Mars–Jupiter).

Mars: We're not trying to make friends here. It's strictly following our brief.

Jupiter: We can't forget that these are people's lives.

Pam: I agree with both of you.

Mercury–Saturn: When's the coffee coming?

Pam: And I know (smiling at Mercury–Saturn) that you are deeply committed to this.

Mercury–Saturn: Absolutely (he smiles at Pam).

Mars: So let's talk.

Pam: Since I'm a temporary addition, would it work best if you used me as a sounding board?

Pamela uses a different sort of communication for each type. She establishes her credentials and allows the aggression of the Mars type to wash over her without responding. She draws the distracted Mercury–Saturn type into the conversation by reminding him of his 'deep commitment'. She leaves it to the Jupiter and Mars–Jupiter types to respond to the Mars type's aggression. Finally, having appeared to be neutral and possibly pliable, she places herself in a central position by offering to be a sounding board. This also means that she does not have to venture her own opinions. She does not have the background information to have formed any and this lack might cause the Mars type energy in the room to attack her credibility.

The Three 'Kinds' of People

Just as we are recognized and separated by our 12-type characteristics, so not all people who come across psychological ideas or an esoteric system react to the ideas or system in the same way.

Person Number One: Has no inner will or driving force. Needs the influence of the teaching in order to fill them up. (We can observe this in mainstream religious practice where some people follow the dictates of their leaders without question or rational discussion.)

Person Number Two: Takes the ideas and *makes use of them for his or her benefit*. (May do this in an informed and constructive way, utilizing a number of systems to form a cohesive inner support. If the individual does not develop, they may engage on the surface with various systems but never understand the deeper purpose of the teachings.)

Person Number Three: *Becomes* the ideas. Lives in the world of the ideas. (A deep adherence to the philosophy and purpose of the teachings. They are devoted to their proper use and increasing their understanding. May in their turn become a teacher.)

To avoid being left with no more than a glancing, or surface, encounter with the 12-type Enneagram, it is helpful to consider this list. Even if we have not until now had a sense of something supportive inside us, we can use the ideas of the Enneagram for inner growth. Even if we are a type-two person in *other* respects – for example, if we have absorbed bits and pieces from other psychological approaches and psychometric tests to help with different elements of our individual needs, but hold no deep adherence to anything – we can still be a type three *in terms of the 12-type Enneagram*. The relevance and applications of the knowledge are limitless: only *our* individual factors will limit their usefulness. On the other hand, if we have already experienced being a three in other circumstances, then we have laid the groundwork for a profound and thorough immersion in this system.

Identifying the Type Influences in our Daily Life

In a previous chapter we saw how the simple, unavoidable, process of rising each morning and beginning our day takes us through at least some of the different type-influences. What is particularly fascinating is to see how much the different type-influences are present, throughout our day.

Here is someone who manifests the different type-energies in a way that is unhelpful to her:

> Dawn is sent on a day's workshop on improving her communicating skills. She arrives late because she has not taken the time to work out the best travel route (Venus-type laziness; Lunar type excuses instead of having accessed proper use of Mercury-type energy). To make up for this, she insists on explaining to the rest of the group the exact reasons for her attendance (wrong use of Lunar- and Mars-type energies).
>
> When the group is finally allowed to move on, because she decides she has received insufficient support and pampering, Dawn glowers at the facilitator (wrong use of Mars-type energy). The facilitator picks up on this and invites Dawn to explain her mood, but Dawn suddenly feels embarrassed and shies away (negative Lunar-type energy). Throughout the day, despite the facilitator's request, Dawn takes phone

calls regarding her car being serviced (wrong use of Mercury-type energy). Mid-afternoon, taking the temperature of the room regarding her performance, she makes a passionate plea for understanding and sympathy (wrong use of Lunar and Venus-type energy). At the end no one wants to give her a hug. Dawn becomes aggressive and storms off (wrong use of Mars-type energy). Driving home, talking on her mobile as she drives, she tells her husband she is feeling devastated that she encountered such negativity, and weeps for herself (negative Venus-type energy).

Dawn accesses various type-energies *but consistently uses them in a negative or inappropriate way.* Dawn turns what could have been a useful day of learning into yet another damaging experience. This example is not an exaggeration. We all know people who seem to 'have a talent' for picking exactly the *wrong* reaction to whatever event they encounter. They are simply using the wrong energy, either unconsciously or, worse, they believe they are doing it 'deliberately'. What is really happening is another form of mechanical unconsciousness: they *can't* do it differently. Exposure to the 12-type Enneagram will be invaluable for anyone who sees, either in themselves or in someone else, the expression of the *wrong type-energy.*

An example where we *accidentally* employ both positive and negative, or appropriate and inappropriate, type-energies, is below.

We are at work, between assignments. We spend a little time on the computer, checking sports scores or celebrity gossip (wrong use of Venus and Mercury-type energy). Our boss suddenly appears, looming over our terminal (panic: negative Lunar-type energy). She wants to give feedback on our last project (paranoia: negative Lunar-type energy). She praises our speed and accuracy (preening: mixed Venus and Mercury-type energy). Just as we relax, she hits us with a fundamental problem concerning the project and we immediately become defensive (wrong use of Mars-type energy). She challenges our thinking (indignation: negative Mars energy and distressed Saturn-type thinking). We strive to get out of the hole (proper use of Mars-type energy). We explain our thinking (proper use of Saturn-type energy).

We bring in other people in the team, who back up our methodology (proper use of Saturn–Mars energy). In order that the boss does not lose face, we make positive responses about her comments (proper use of Jupiter-type energy).

The imaginary person in this example has learned enough regarding what is necessary in office politics to know how to deal with their boss. This does not mean, however, that this is a person functioning 'consciously'. The earlier description, with the panoply of one energy after another coursing through the person's thoughts and feelings, indicates that although *this time* things worked out, the next time might be different.

Wasting and Conserving Essence Energy

Energy, obviously, is not limitless. Therefore it behoves us to think about, and place more value on, the energy we have, and think about how this energy is divided up inside us, either consciously or unconsciously. We have probably all had the experience of needing to do something but thinking 'I just don't have the energy.' If we leave it for a while, when we attempt the project later we find we now do have the energy. This shows that energy is not always freely available, and that we need a *particular* type of energy for a particular task.

Each type wastes its precious essence energy in its own way.

Lunar type: Clouds of unreal/spacy thoughts and fantasies. Imagining things that are not going to happen – and becoming frightened, panicked, depressed or experiencing some other negative emotion over these invented thoughts.

Lunar–Venus type: Spend valuable energy pursuing profitless emotional intrigues. Energy is better used building up some reality and self-reliance in their lives (saving for a rainy day; nurturing supportive non-sexual friendships).

Venus type: Obsessive interest in the lives of celebrities and over-involvement in soaps and reality TV.

Venus–Mercury type: Pursues friendships and activities that have little point or profit.

Mercury type: Inability to 'stop' movement. Constant twitching, restless pacing and foot tapping. Their minds run three or four incomplete streams of thought at once. Useless information that further confuses.

Mercury–Saturn type: Waste their thought and speed influences on profitless pursuits.

Saturn type: Meaningless intellectualism. Reading/writing books that twist and turn themselves inside out and become exhausting and valueless. Unnecessarily pedantic attitudes that expend energy through fruitless debate and argument.

Saturn–Mars type: Marshal their formidable talents to an unworthy aim, for example Joan Crawford's manic scheming undermining her admirable achievements.

Mars type: Unnecessary point scoring and manipulation of events and people, ostensibly for a purpose but actually only because the type-energy is not being properly managed.

Mars–Jupiter type: Stop trying to make converts when it is not going to lead to anything. Recognize that some people do not want to be 'saved'.

Jupiter type: Useless and meaningless agonizing over events we cannot do anything about. This is different from being galvanized into action: that is admirable. But Jupiter energy used for valueless 'suffering', which is not then channelled appropriately, is a waste.

Jupiter–Lunar type: Consign themselves to 'bridesmaid' or 'best friend' role and tell themselves they are doing something worthwhile 'anyway'.

Chapter 18

Why the 12-Type Enneagram Is So Crucial

A recent newspaper article about Narcissistic Personality Disorder offers an example of why it would help humankind generally for there to be more understanding of the presence, and the consequences, of the planetary-ray influences. The symptoms of the disorder include a lack of empathy, exaggerated self-belief and self-aggrandisement, and a disregard for others. It is possible to interpret these symptoms as a deranged, psychotic version of Saturn–Mars type, recognizable, in its most extreme manifestation, in Hitler. Although it would be simplistic to say that merely by diagnosing 'wrong use of planetary ray influences' some forms of mental illness will be immediately cured, it is an indication of how powerful and widespread are the consequences of influences about which the general population is unaware and uninformed. By becoming more conscious of how we, and others, operate in terms of the alchemical effects of planetary force centres, we become more able to work with the predictable consequences of the essence energies, rather than mechanically acting out unconsciously.

Intellectual, Emotional and Physical Responsibility

We each have areas where we are stronger or weaker. G I Gurdjieff offered the categories of Man No. 1, the physical, Man No. 2 the emotional and Man No. 3 the intellectual. In terms of the 12-type Enneagram, our *type limitations* are the reason why we lack in one or another centre. The list below indicates the principal areas in which each type needs to make conscious efforts in order to achieve strength in all three areas:

Lunar type: Emotional. Plus developing thinking in Saturn-type depth rather than Lunar-type scattiness.

Venus type: Intellectual. Plus developing sufficient speed (moving centre).

Mercury type: Emotional and intellectual. Plus slowing down in the moving centre.

Saturn type: Emotional and moving.

Mars type: Emotional, in the sense of caring for others. Plus using physical and intellectual qualities positively and responsibly, not caught up in the fierce drives of this energy.

Jupiter type: Moving, some intellectual, emotional. Working on the self responsibly, not allowing outside demands to be an excuse.

Becoming a Good Example of our Type

When we begin to study the 12-type Enneagram we cannot expect anything else than that up till this point we have been unconsciously defaulting; we have been operating out of type; we have, with unawareness, been drawing from the beneficial twin type; and we have generally been bouncing unconsciously round the Enneagram, sometimes beneficially, sometimes to our detriment.

Becoming a good example of our type means firstly determining where we are, and secondly beginning to let go of aspects of what we previously thought of as our 'personality': all the consequences of defaulting, bouncing around unconsciously, and so on.

We can be helped in this by a number of processes.

- We can take 'snapshots' of how we are in any given situation. Given our type, are we helping ourselves to grow and develop into a good example? Or are we being too indulgent, flying off the handle, not being responsible, using speed as a substitute for thought? This should not be the starting point for us to feel bad or punish ourselves. It is far too easy to put ourselves down. The point here is not criticism, it is only *to see what is*. We take the snapshot, it tells us something about ourselves, and we seek, through thinking, planning and experimenting, to refine and improve our subsequent thoughts, feelings or behaviour. Obviously when we begin it is not as easy to do this as it will be once we are used to regarding ourselves from the perspective of our 12-type Enneagram type. This in itself gives us an exciting new opportunity for exploration into our inner processes and how we can positively influence ourselves, and others.

- We can ask friends and appropriate work colleagues for feedback. Again, here the idea is not to give people *carte blanche* to criticize us, but other people can see things about us that they would never think to tell us, but that we would gain by hearing.
- We can, at the end of each day, review the day in terms of the quality we have brought to it. The idea is to see ourselves as being involved in a fascinating exploration, and to see all the days of our lives as an ongoing opportunity to improve, refine and increase our ability to utilize the particular qualities of our essence type.

As people around us are exposed to the ideas of the 12-type Enneagram, so they become an invaluable source of information for us. We can do the same for the people we know, always remembering to offer the information tentatively, as though we are both taking part in an experiment, the goal of which is always some aspect of greater, more honest or more appropriate understanding of us and themselves.

Striving to Access Higher Type-Energy

Within the relentless pace of a day, or in a moment of haste, we tend to operate in 'survival' mode; we often throw out the bare minimum of a response. This is understandable, and it lies on the opposite end of the line to a response that invokes the rich essence of our type. We should strive at least to be cognizant of the higher form of our type-energy.

Of course, this means something different for each of the types, and this is not an easy task. If we imagine that when we first encounter the 12-type Enneagram, we have already had many years of unconsciously bouncing round the various types, we will inevitably have 'ways' of reacting that are not adding to our type essence, but weakening it. By consciously seeking to be a good representative of our type we attain a *more objective understanding* of the 12-type Enneagram influences.

For those of us who are hybrid types, the challenge remains the same: to strive to understand and live by consciously accessing the energy influences appropriate to our type. This may not mean *separating* the two energy influences, but understanding the result of the dual influences, and seeking to employ both these influences more consciously and effectively. We should always remember that the importance of understanding and working with the essence energies is that *we get what we most need right in our home energy*: yet we often go everywhere else, and do everything we can to distract ourselves, rather than accepting the real and appropriate help we can always access by turning inward and becoming more attuned to our type-energy.

Using the Enneagram to Understand and Help Others
What Sort of Person Should We Be?

Should we all be aiming for the same goal? Once we have encountered the 12-type Enneagram, with its clearly defined and designated path for spiritual progression and alchemical transformation, do we all find fulfilment, ultimately, in the same place? This would mean that, wherever we began, we should all be aiming to acquire Jupiter-type manifestation. There are some interesting examples where even a type as self-focused as the pure Venus type can, through a conscious desire, transform themselves into living a Jupiter-type life. Elizabeth Taylor, the very epitome of the languid lover, moved from self-absorption to working tirelessly and selflessly to bring awareness of AIDS to the general public.

The true answer is to be found in the nature of the various energies. Elizabeth Taylor *did* evolve, but she evolved *in terms of her Venus-type nature*. We must remember that each of the energies understands everything in its own way. Therefore Taylor's sincerely manifested Jupiter-type energy was the Venus type's understanding of Jupiter-type energy. Therefore, wherever we begin, we can use the conscious manifestations of the Jupiter energy in order to complete our journey (as we would going through the Enneagram diagram), knowing that we are not attempting to become a Jupiter type as would a Jupiter type themselves, but instead bringing about our own self-fulfilment by living life in our type's understanding of Jupiter type.

Characteristics of Developed Essence Types

Much of the focus of this book has been on observing the *undeveloped* aspects of each type-energy. However, it would be a weak system if there were not abundant examples of developed types. Obviously, once an individual has encountered the 12-type Enneagram they can then consciously access and explore their own, the beneficial forward energy type, and all the other types:

Lunar type: Here the positive aspects in terms of creativity, enthusiasm, loyalty and kindness integrate with the warmth and one-to-one abilities of Venus type. We would also find a useful application of Mercury-type energy for organization and task-completion, the ability to develop thought trains and patterns properly in Saturn type, an awareness of the need to self-protect using Mars-type energy and a genuine expression of concern towards others that is the presence of Jupiter-type energy.

Venus type: Here the positive aspects of warmth, sensuousness and one-to-one listening are enhanced by the individual's ability to get things done using Mercury energy, have a certain intellectual capacity gained by accessing Saturn type, and an ability to protect and promote the self while not putting others down which would be a combination of Mars and Jupiter type.

Mercury type: Here the positive aspects of speed, organization and completing tasks are enhanced by an ability to think things through at a sophisticated level, while they manage situations using Mars-type energy, have a well-balanced access to Jupiter energy and are amusing and popular using Lunar-type energy.

Saturn type: Here the positive aspects of profound and original thinking join with an ability to make things happen using Mars-type energy, with a genuine concern for others coming from Jupiter type, a needed lightness from Lunar-type energy and the ability to function emotionally coming from Venus type.

Mars type: Here the positive aspects of a powerful presence and ability to manage and take responsibility are joined with a true Jupiter-type compassion for others and a desire to promote worthwhile work. This combines with a charming Lunar-type lightness, Venus-type's ability to be sensuous and present in a one-to-one relationship and Mercury-type's organizational skills.

Jupiter type: Here the positive aspects of sincere dedication to others and abundantly flowing good-will join with a delightful lightness from Lunar type, the ability to create an intimate relationship from Venus type, the organization and productive busy-ness of Mercury type, the depth of Saturn type and the uncompromising boldness and toughness of Mars type.

As previously noted, hybrid types contain the influence of two consecutive energy types as well as being a unique result of the blend. There would be too much repetition to list the qualities of developed hybrids. From your reading you will be able to make these connections yourself.

Bringing the Right Conscious Energy to Situations

Whatever our essence type, we can bring a specific type-energy to situations. Here are some examples, where the person is actually a Saturn type:

Lunar type: I go into this energy (or rather, my under-standing of this type-energy) when I am seeing something for the first time. For example, when I arrive at a new holiday destination. I don't want to fall into the trap of comparing the new city with others I have already visited. So I use Lunar-type energy really to open my eyes and drink in the unfamiliar impressions.

I also use Lunar-type energy when I do not want to be jaded. When I have heard a piece of music many times, this energy helps me experience the music afresh. I use it also when I want to *wonder* about a question, when I want to meander in it and allow intuitive thoughts to go where they will.

Venus type: The best way for me to understand this type is to identify Venus-type friends and see how they experience the world. Then I attempt to find this experience in myself.

I also use Venus-type energy when I need to understand someone's emotional journey. In this energy I want to know every emotional twist and turn. Here I also experience the pleasure of shutting off my intellectual responses and just going with the reactions of my body and my senses.

Mercury type: Saturn type has come from Mercury type and I do not find it difficult to access this energy consciously. I have observed that my thinking is most free when my study is neatly organized and so I consciously put aside time to deal with ever-mounting paperwork.

I also use this energy when I have to research buying something new. I don't want to become too involved in Saturn-type investigations: in Mercury type I cover the greatest amount of ground in the least time.

Saturn type: Given type-blindness, I am usually not conscious of actually being in my own essence type. Occasionally it comes as a surprise to remember that not everyone sees the world as I do. Yet I would never wish to be another type since the depth of understanding this energy makes available to me is an ongoing pleasure and fascination.

Mars type: I know that this is the type-energy I need to learn most about. I find that being bold is not in my nature, yet I also appreciate that learning how to manifest this energy consciously has been an enormous help in overcoming my natural 'shyness' and introversion.

I use this energy when I need to stand up for myself. Also when I have got into a rut and need to cut out unprofitable activities, whether they be with friends who drain me or unproductive work.

Jupiter type: I use Jupiter type to make sense of where I should place my energy. Here I am reminded that life is limited and our best choices are those that benefit others.

I also use this energy when faced with a difficult or unpleasant situation. For example, unexpectedly encountering a neighbour with whom I have had troubled dealings in the past, I could go into Mars type but by choosing Jupiter-type energy I can greet them with genuine pleasure and warmth that turns the negative positive.

While setting down these notes I experienced a perfect example of why we should all strive to manifest appropriate Jupiter-type energy consciously. This is regardless of whether or not our overall goal is to move into a permanent Jupiter-type energy state. I was at the front of the queue at the bank to pay in a large cheque. A woman appeared asking if anyone was just paying in cheques. I said yes and she encouraged me to follow her, so I left my place. She indicated the electronic pay-in teller. I said I wanted the funds cleared as soon as possible and she said the electronic teller did this, and left me. *At the back of the queue for the electronic teller.*

I looked back to my place in the queue. The person behind me was being served. I waited in the queue and finally made the deposit. The woman was still standing around looking helpful, so when I left I thought should I say something? I had some irritation so I spoke to her *in conscious Jupiter-type energy*. I found myself spontaneously laughing while I mentioned to her that I had been at the front of the queue and she had led me to the back of the other one. She apologized and I continued to laugh merrily. Which, since this was a small irritation, was entirely appropriate. Had I gone into Mars-type fire not only would she have been upset but I would have stayed in the energy for a long time (it is difficult not to). There are of course many, many larger and important examples of selecting the right energy. This is included *because* it is a small, everyday, easy to overlook example of *making a conscious choice* and not falling into a mechanical default.

It also is an example of how the wisdom of the 12-type Enneagram is not 'unworldly', 'spiritual', 'superior': it can help us each and every moment, in the largest to the smallest aspects of our day.

Reviewing the Important Milestones of your Life

Looking back on your life, what would you have said or done differently if you had had the wisdom of the 12-type Enneagram?

- How would your schooling have been different?
- How would you have gone about finding someone to love?

- How would you have understood and dealt with your parents or parent?
- On which friendships would you have worked harder?
- Would you make different career choices?
- Should you have travelled? Or not travelled so much?
- Should you have settled down?
- Could you have made peace with being single?

It is not an exaggeration to state that there is no single aspect of your life which would not have been affected or influenced by your knowing the 12-type Enneagram before you started out. You may wonder why it is in life that so much of the knowledge that is taught in education is never applied, and that knowledge such as this, with direct, meaningful application, is obviously unknown.

All that we can know is that up till this time, the information has been hidden. Only now, at this point in history, are the keys being offered, and we will gain most from sincerely and gratefully accepting the gift of these keys, dwelling not on what we could have done, but what we are now on the threshold of exploring.

A Last Addition from my Teacher

'The main task in life is to *enter fully* and *fully refine* your *essence-type* characteristics. It works in sequence. You have to:

1. Get out of the *false characteristics* of your type. For example, for Lunar type this might be doing a guided meditation. If the Lunar type is told just to 'sit there' it would not have been successful because Lunar types, like children, function best when they have *a defined task*. So a guided meditation helps to strengthen the Lunar type ray and releases the Lunar type for a time from the Mercury ray (many Lunar types go into a skewed type of Mercury ray which they believe is helpful. It is to some extent but it also deprives the Lunar type of their type's intuitive sense).

2. Once the faulty identification with other types has given way to your *own essence type*, then you can work on it and also, to some extent, on other-type characteristics which we have to have. Again, for example, a Lunar type *can* benefit from Mercury-type energy, but this should be the

version that is balanced by the other two signs before it. Thus the sequence is Lunar-type intuition, then towards slower Venus-type self-care, then forward to benefit from Mercury type. Mercury type, accessed by Lunar type, also needs to be balanced by the deep reasoning ability of Saturn type.

3. When it is fairly clear how you function – for good or bad – in *all* the type-energies – they you examine how you have gone round the 12-type Enneagram and how you can profit from going, *in order*, around it from the present moment onward.

4. Then, you notice the moments in your life when you have been going correctly round the Enneagram and have *crossed* some of the inner lines connecting two types, or lines related to the *karmic forces* of numbers 3, 6 and 9. Seek to understand what happened to you at that juncture. By this you realize what is in store for future trips and *try to manage the shocks consciously.*

'One important observation is that natural (not domesticated, highly 'bred') *animals* exist in a fairly unchangeable type-straitjacket: entire *families* of animals share certain characteristics even though the various species have completely different ways of expressing the major links. The entire *cat* family has links to Venus type (lounge a lot, but powerful when they go in for the kill). Dogs descend from various Mars-type influences and Mars type likes routine, likes to follow rules, and make others follow them.

'Birds, butterflies and flying things are Lunar type primarily, but there are many variations: from eagle to hummingbird. They, like Lunar types, are easily distracted, but when they 'zero in' on something, they are oblivious to everything else. (The eagle can see a mouse from far away and seems to be Mars type, rather than Lunar type. This is true, but as a flying thing, it does not travel in packs, or lounge around. It has the restlessness of Lunar types.)

'*People* are the species *capable of change*, and therefore *not* born into as rigid type-characteristics as animals are. The clearest indication of this is vocalization: men and women can make sounds like any one of the types – no animal can do this . A cat cannot suddenly bark.'

Avoid Becoming an Instant Expert

This warning has already been given. It is repeated at this final stage of the book's journey. There is a tendency in all of us to snatch a few ideas out of a system and believe we know enough to tell others. My teacher reports that *his* teachers said that *'for each piece of information we tell someone else, we should know a hundred pieces of information ourselves'*. It is not the purpose of this book to create instant experts in the 12-type Enneagram. The wisdom and importance of the ideas are best understood through long reflection and careful observation of both ourselves and others. A shallow or incomplete understanding robs us of the greater purpose and value of the Enneagram. We gain by taking time and reflection before sharing our observations. This sharing should always be done with respect; when we respect something or someone, we also respect ourselves and the deeper parts of our own selves will open and connect with our ordinary consciousness.

The Wisdom of the 12-Type Enneagram

The wisdom of the 12-type Enneagram is 'old'. For centuries it has survived only as the most esoteric of knowledge systems. Who can say exactly why this book is *now* being written? This book is the first time the existence of the 12-type Enneagram has been shared with the world. This means that this is a crucial moment in the development of understanding. Will the movement of growth and development, in accordance with the cycle of the six main energies, be harmonious, progressive and finally, triumphant?

Or will it be seized on by the 'wrong' sort of recipient, abused and exploited, and finally, possibly with a sense of immense satisfaction from those self-same exploitative exponents, rejected as 'not as amazing as we thought it was'? All this would mean is that they have entirely missed the opportunity for understanding, transformation, and even possibly redemption. The wisdom will continue to survive in the way that nothing of value is truly *entirely* lost, but it may again become lost to a wider audience. Therefore we must approach the ideas, and the information the ideas have for us, with respect, integrity and responsibility. Remember that it is said that it is better not to attempt to develop psychologically or spiritually rather than to develop in the wrong way which will *worsen* our situation. We must take care that this does not happen with our exposure to the 12-type Enneagram.

The End is the Beginning

Interpreted and applied with care, respect and sincerity, the 12-type Enneagram will become a positive force in every aspect of our daily lives. We can use the information to better our own quality of life, to illuminate work and relationship issues, and to understand other people in a deeper and more meaningful way. The end of reading this book is the beginning of launching ourselves on a powerful, mysterious and exciting journey of self-investigation, from now and for the rest of our lives.

Index

WATKINS

Sharing Wisdom Since
1893

The story of Watkins Publishing dates back to March 1893, when John M. Watkins, a scholar of esotericism, overheard his friend and teacher Madame Blavatsky lamenting the fact that there was nowhere in London to buy books on mysticism, occultism or metaphysics. At that moment Watkins was born, soon to become the home of many of the leading lights of spiritual literature, including Carl Jung, Rudolf Steiner, Alice Bailey and Chögyam Trungpa.

Today our passion for vigorous questioning is still resolute. With over 350 titles on our list, Watkins Publishing reflects the development of spiritual thinking and new science over the past 120 years. We remain at the cutting edge, committed to publishing books that change lives.

DISCOVER MORE ...

| Read our blog | Watch and listen to our authors in action | Sign up to our mailing list |

JOIN IN THE CONVERSATION

 WatkinsPublishing   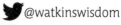@watkinswisdom

 WatkinsPublishingLtd   +watkinspublishing1893

Our books celebrate conscious, passionate, wise and happy living.
Be part of the community by visiting

www.watkinspublishing.com